STUDIES IN ARTHUR SCHNITZLER

UNIVERSITY OF NORTH CAROLINA
STUDIES IN THE GERMANIC LANGUAGES
AND LITERATURES

Number Forty-two

UNIVERSITY
OF NORTH CAROLINA
STUDIES IN
THE GERMANIC LANGUAGES
AND LITERATURES

STUDIES IN ARTHUR SCHNITZLER

CENTENNIAL COMMEMORATIVE VOLUME

Edited by

HERBERT W. REICHERT

and

HERMAN SALINGER

AMS PRESS INC.
New York
1966

INTRODUCTION

In April, 1961, the *International Arthur Schnitzler Research Association* was founded during, though not as a function of, the fourteenth annual University of Kentucky Foreign Language Conference at Lexington. The principal purpose of the IASRA is implicit in its name. With the late Dr. Bruno Walter as Chairman of the Board of Honorary Directors, the organization started with some seventy-five members in thirteen countries and has grown since then by more than 75%, a fact that contributes convincingly to the steadily mounting evidence of a vigorous Schnitzler-Renaissance. As the first anniversary of the IASRA coincided with the Schnitzler Centennial, the IASRA asked for and received permission to organize a special Arthur Schnitzler Centennial Section as part of the fifteenth UKFL Conference.

After some twenty-five Schnitzler-scholars had been contacted, there emerged a slate of eight papers which were read by their authors at the University of Kentucky on April 27, 1962. The meeting, under the chairmanship of Professor Herman Salinger of Duke University, Secretary-Treasurer of the IASRA, was very well attended, and since the comments of a discriminating audience were most favorable, the idea of publishing the eight papers together as a *Festschrift* seemed only logical and was indeed advanced by several of those present.

The manuscripts were then collected by Professor Salinger and edited by Professor Herbert W. Reichert of the University of North Carolina, Vice President of the IASRA.

Thus the IASRA became the proud godfather of a rather unusual memorial volume. Its most unorthodox features are probably the lack of eulogistic verbiage and of reverently exhumed odds and ends ascribed to Schnitzler's pen. Not only do we present, instead, eight original essays, based on scholarly inquiry into widely diverging aspects of the poet's work, but several of their authors come from academic fields other than that of Germanics, *i.e.*, from History (Professor Kann), English (Professor Spector), and Library Sciences (Dr. Dayag).

There is nothing to be gained by discussing the contributions individually. We prefer to let the reader himself, unaided by editorial tutelage (*caveat lector!*), examine these studies of Arthur Schnitzler's work which today, over three decades after his death, appears to be better understood and appreciated than ever before.

Autumn 1963, Lexington, Ky.

ROBERT O. WEISS
President, IASRA

CONTENTS

ARTHUR SCHNITZLERS UNVERÖFFENTLICHTE TRAGIKOMÖDIE *DAS WORT*

Von Kurt Bergel

Das Wort

Vom steilen Weg ist Lipp' und Herz verdorrt,
Doch endlich lohnt ein wundersam Gelingen:
Der Wahrheit Tempel ragt am heil'gen Ort.
Da dröhnt es aus dem Dunkel: Weiche fort!
Hier wird kein Sterblicher sich Einlass zwingen,-
Ein Riese hält am Tore Wacht: *das Wort.*

ARTHUR SCHNITZLER (Aus dem Nachlass)

In diesem Jahre der hundertsten Wiederkehr seines Geburtstages feiern wir Arthur Schnitzler, wie es uns als Germanisten gemäss ist: durch kritische Deutung seines Werkes wollen wir zur Einsicht in seine Dichtung und sein Dichtertum beitragen. Doch indem wir einen Grossen zu ehren suchen, ehren wir mehr noch uns selbst, – wenigstens solange wir nicht der Hybris des Literaturwissenschaftlers verfallen, uns aus dienenden Deutern des Dichtwerks zu dessen selbstherrlichen Richtern aufzuwerfen.

Zu seinen Lebzeiten war Schnitzler innigst geliebt von einer Generation, die sich in den Gestalten vor allem seiner Frühwerke wiedererkannte, und zugleich gehasst von anderen, die – sei es aus hinterwäldlerischer Enge oder aus ehrlichem Missverstehen – sich ein verzerrtes Bild, ja manchmal eine Karikatur des nicht immer einfachen Menschen und in Literaturkategorien nicht leicht einzuordnenden Dichters zusammenpinselten. War der junge Schnitzler Sprecher einer Avantgarde, so erschien der alternde Dichter manchen als Zeuge einer „versunkenen Welt."

Wie aber steht es heute, da die Zäsur dieser Jahrhundertsfeier uns die Frage nach seiner Stellung und Geltung be-

1

sonders dringend vorlegt? Die Antwort hierauf kann nicht die Aufgabe dessen sein, der auf stark begrenztem Raum von einem bisher unbekannt gebliebenen Werk des Dichters berichten will. Nur so viel möchte ich sagen: Als 1918 Schnitzler die Gesammelten Werke von Alfred Kerr gelesen hatte, schrieb er diesem: „'Recht haben' wie wenig bedeutet das im Grunde, da ja die entgiltige Entscheidung doch erst in unserer Abwesenheit gefällt wird und auch dann noch nicht entgiltig sein dürfte."[1] Schnitzler schrieb diese Worte zu Beginn der Epoche, in der es Mode werden sollte, sein dichterisches Werk als Anachronismus zu belächeln, weil es – im Gegensatz zu der „aktuelleren" Produktion der Nachkriegsliteratur – sich „nur" mit solchen Problemen wie Liebe und Hass, Leben und Tod zu beschäftigen schien. Gewiss, die „entgiltige Entscheidung" über Schnitzler war 1918 noch nicht fällig, und zu jeder Zeit wird sie nur bedingt gefällt werden dürfen. Doch wir, in des Dichters „Abwesenheit," mögen uns an eine spätere Stelle des gleichen Briefes halten, in der Schnitzler dies über die Geltung eines Werkes sagt: „Sein und Wirken ist alles."

Heute, 31 Jahre nach des Dichters Tod, da dem Leser und Theaterbesucher sein Werk in neuer Sicht und dem Forscher überdies ein reicher Nachlass von Unveröffentlichtem vorliegt, spricht Schnitzlers „Sein und Wirken" lebendig und stark zu uns. Die Älteren unter uns, je nach Alter und Herkunft, teilen zwar noch bis zu einem gewissen Grade das Erlebnis von Schnitzlers Welt, doch zugleich sind wir alle durch das Inferno des zwölfjährigen Selbstmordes und das Purgatorio des wiedererstehenden Europas von ihr tief geschieden. Wenden wir uns aus der Perspektive unserer Zeit seinem Werke wieder zu, so erscheint es überraschend frisch, manchmal prophetisch, selten naiv, zwar nicht immer von höchstem dichterischem Rang, doch meist faszinierend und fast nie belanglos.

Da ja noch immer das geradezu legendär gewordene Bild von Schnitzler dem Playboy des franz-josephinischen Wien oder dem dekadenten Erotomanen unter den Menschen spukt, fordert die Gerechtigkeit, dass man es ausspricht, wie anders er dem vorurteilsfreien Leser seines Gesamtwerks im Rückblick erscheint: als ein Dichter, dessen psychologischer Tief- und Spürsinn, angetrieben von rücksichtsloser Wahrheitsliebe, dem Menschenbild der Literatur am Ende des neunzehnten und im ersten Drittel des zwanzigsten Jahrhunderts eine neue Vielschichtigkeit gegeben hat. Wir sehen einen Menschen, der es aus der inneren Unruhe eines nach Neuland Strebenden und aus Hass gegen Bequemlichkeit ablehnt, sich über sich selbst und andere täuschen zu lassen und der so ein Wegweiser durch das Dschungel der Seele im Zeitalter der Tiefenpsychologie geworden ist.

Unter den zahlreichen Entwürfen, die sich in Schnitzlers Nachlass befinden, ist eine bisher unbekannt gebliebene Tragikomödie, *Das Wort*, von besonderem Interesse. Das Werk liegt uns in mehreren Fassungen und zahlreichen Skizzen vor, doch keine Version befriedigte Schnitzler, den anspruchsvollen Kritiker seiner selbst; in jahrelanger Arbeit gelang es ihm nicht, dieses Stück abzurunden und abzuschliessen.[2] An Zeit und Lust hat es ihm nicht gefehlt. Die ersten Notizen über *Das Wort* gehen in das Jahr 1904 zurück, und die letzten Arbeiten an dem weit fortgeschrittenen Manuskript stammen aus dem Jahr 1927.[3] Nicht alle vorhandenen Entwürfe sind datiert, doch lässt sich mit Sicherheit sagen, dass der Dichter in mindestens neun der dreiundzwanzig Jahre das Stück aufgegriffen, weitergeführt und wieder zur Seite gelegt hat. Mehr noch: er war 1906 so weit gediehen, dass für ihn „über den Sinn der Gestalten, über den Geist ihrer gegenseitigen Beziehungen... kein Zweifel mehr" bestand; er konnte das Stück Otto Brahm zur Aufführung am Deutschen Theater in Aussicht stellen.[4] Aus den Manuskripten geht überdies hervor, dass Schnitzler am 18. Mai 1907 in Anwesenheit seiner Frau Otto Brahm das Fragment des Stücks vorgelesen hatte; er notierte danach im einzelnen, was er für die Stärken und Schwächen seiner Tragikomödie hielt, endete aber seine Bemerkungen mit den Worten „Vorläufig weg damit." Doch reizte die Arbeit ihn immer wieder, und 1927 lag *Das Wort* schliesslich als ein Fragment vor, das aus mehr abgeschlossenen als unfertigen Szenen besteht. Es ist diese Fassung letzter Hand, auf die ich mich im folgenden stütze.

Der erste Akt führt uns in ein schäbiges Wiener Kaffeehaus – „eigentlich besseres Tschecherl," – in dem hauptsächlich Literaten und Strassenmädchen verkehren. Im Mittelpunkt dieses Kreises steht Anastasius Treuenhof, der von den Schriftstellern wie den Dirnen seines Stammlokals gleichermassen als genialer Dichter und Mensch verehrt und als Original nachgeahmt wird. Kürzlich hat Treuenhof für eines der Mädchen, Albine, einen Liebesbrief an den Komödiendichter Gleissner geschrieben, – eine Art von Variation einer Episode im *Cyrano de Bergerac*. Unter den neuen Besuchern dieses Lokals ist an jenem Abend Frau Flatterer, eine Berlinerin, deren Gedichtband den anspruchsvollen Titel „Keusche Räusche" trägt. Sie will für Treuenhof, der – von seinem Vaterland vernachlässigt – Not leidet, eine Hilfsaktion organisieren.[5] Zum Treuenhofkreis gehört auch ein eleganter Schneider, van Zack, der von seinen Freunden als „Reform-Kultur-Kostümkünstler" geschätzt wird. Er bringt seine junge hübsche Frau Lisa heute zum ersten Mal in das zweideutige Kaffeehaus mit, denn Treuenhof hat ihm eingeredet, dass man „eine Frau nicht kennt, ehe sich nicht jeder Winkel der Welt in ihren Augen gespiegelt hat. Und man besitzt eine Frau nicht, ehe man sie kennt."[6] Da tritt der junge, gerade aus Italien zurückgekommene Maler Willi Langer ein, und vom ersten Augenblick an fühlen er und Lisa sich zueinander hingezogen. Gleissner wittert hier eine Gelegenheit, sich dafür zu rächen, dass Lisa ihn einmal zurückgewiesen hatte; er schlägt vor, Willi solle Lisas Porträt malen. Die beiden gehen auf diesen Vorschlag voller Eifer ein.

Der zweite Akt spielt im Wohnzimmer von Frau Langer, der

4

verwitweten Mutter des Malers. Sie ist eine jener vorurteilsfreien Frauenrechtlerinnen, wie wir sie zuerst in Ibsens
Stücken und bei Schnitzler in Gestalten wie der Emma Winter
im *Vermächtnis* finden. Mit Hilfe ihres Bruders, des Hofrats
Winkler, ist sie im Begriffe, ein Heim für uneheliche Kinder zu
gründen. „Der schwere Duft von Verstehen in diesem Haus,"
heisst es in einer Skizze Schnitzlers zu diesem Akt. Vor vielen
Jahren liebte Frau Langer Treuenhof, heiratete jedoch einen
gutbürgerlichen Mann. Noch immer trägt sie das Bild des
jungen genialen und warmherzigen Treuenhof im Herzen und
kann sich selbst nicht ganz zugeben, dass Treuenhof jetzt nur
noch ein Schatten seines früheren Selbst ist. Sie will dem
mittellosen Dichter durch eine Art von Sekretärstellung in ihrer
neuen Wohlfahrtsorganisation einen finanziellen Halt schaffen;
er soll gelegentlich Aufrufe für öffentliche Sammlungen
schreiben. Doch Treuenhof weicht aus: „Ich schreib höchstens
im Kaffeehaus auf Marmorplatten, wenn mir zufällig was ein-
fällt." Willi hat Lisa zu malen begonnen. Er gesteht seiner
Mutter, dass er Lisa liebt und dass sie ihren Mann verlassen
und ihn heiraten wird. Die Mutter fürchtet die Eifersucht van
Zacks, doch versucht sie umsonst, Willi von seinem Plan ab-
zubringen.

Der dritte Akt ist wohl der dramatisch beste des Stückes. Im
Dienste seiner Idee, „die Welt aus ihrer grauen Verzauberung
zu erlösen" und sie „wieder bunt zu machen," veranstaltet der
Kunstschneider ein Kostümfest in seinem Atelier, in dem die
Herren in farbigen Fräcken und Kniehosen erscheinen, – eine
echte Jugendstilidee aus dem Vorkriegsjahrzehnt des *art
nouveau*. Unter den Gästen befinden sich Gleissner, der jetzt
mit der früheren Dirne lebt, die Berliner Lyrikerin im Kostüm
einer Bacchantin und einige „Jünger" Treuenhofs. Immer
wieder treffen sich Willi und Lisa im Gewimmel der tanzenden
Gäste, von Lisas Gatten misstrauisch beobachtet. Der von
Grund auf saubere und wahrheitsliebende Willi drängt Lisa,
offen von ihrem Mann ihre Freiheit zu fordern; Lisa aber

zögert, findet eine Ausrede nach der anderen. Treuenhof überzeugt van Zack, er habe die Pflicht, Lisa sich frei entscheiden zu lassen. Van Zack sagt ihr, dass er auf vierzehn Tage verreise, während derer sie Willi nicht sehen soll, damit sie sich allein darüber klar werde, wen sie wirklich liebt. Lisa lügt Willi vor, ihr Mann habe sie nicht freigegeben; es sei alles aus zwischen ihnen. Dann, plötzlich in seinen Armen, verspricht sie ihm ein letztes Zusammensein am folgenden Tag.

Der nächste Akt spielt zwei Wochen später in Willis Atelier. Seit ihres Mannes Abreise ist Lisa Willis Geliebte geworden und hat ihn täglich in seinem Atelier besucht. Nun wird van Zacks Rückkehr erwartet; wieder besteht Willi auf einer offenen Aussprache; er will noch am gleichen Abend abreisen, und Lisa soll ihm folgen, sobald sie sich von ihrem Mann getrennt hat. Kaum hat sie das Atelier verlassen, so erscheint van Zack. Er war schon am vorigen Abend von seiner Reise zurückgekehrt. Lisa hatte ihm versichert, sie habe Willi seit dem Kostümfest nicht mehr gesehen. „Ich hab ihr beinahe schon geglaubt – mehr als das, nicht beinahe. In dieser Nacht war es schwer, ihr nicht zu glauben. Nicht wahr, sie macht es einem schwer, an ihrer Liebe zu zweifeln?" Willi weiss nun, dass Lisa nie die Absicht hatte, die Sicherheit ihres luxuriösen Heims mit einem Leben an der Seite des unfertigen Malers zu vertauschen, dass sie ihn ebenso wie ihren Mann belogen hat. Er ist vernichtet. In unsäglichem Schmerz zerstört er Lisas Bild, das er gemalt hat. Da tritt Treuenhof ein. Mit der psychologischen Blindheit des Egoisten missversteht er die Lage vollständig; tragische Ironie ist es, dass er Lisas Liebe noch immer für echt hält. Doch dann verkündet er mit der ihm eigenen Mischung von arroganter Selbstsicherheit und Selbstkritik:

> Wer darf sagen, ich bin sicher, keine zweite Erbärmlichkeit zu begehen? Nur wer an der ersten zugrunde ging... Woran geh ich zugrunde? Daran,

6

roblematik des
Ohnmacht, mit
Als Beispiel für
Vort gegenüber-
tieftragischen
en Erkennens.
rzichtet, ihren
Tochter zu er-
t steht in un-
ungslosen, das

Notiz der 21.
od und Leben
hinzugefügte
g hin, die er
komödie sah:
enhof seinen
en, so sehr er
orten. Es ist
ikers haben,
dass sein ge-
: Psychologie

der zahlrei-
ritte die hier
gedeutet. Es
viele Züge
der Wiener
ndertwende
Auge. Die
Liebhaber,
eiben lässt,
sch für den
rauen und
zückendste

krepiert bin. Gott
ihr eigenes Leben
zu sterben.

Ich weiss, was ich zu tun

tterers Vorsitz der Verein
ündet werden. Auch ein
ienen; zwar hat er keine
ist, doch verkündet er
Regierung wird sich ihrer
Stück steigert sich jetzt zu
ontrapunkt. Lisa wird zu
e Willi gesagt, dass man
Abstieg ein Ende bereiten
ründungsversammlung des
en lächerlich-pseudo-heroi-
Welt ein „grosses Beispiel"
der Welt scheide: „Wie ein
Dasein vollendet vor uns...
inken, wie es Sokrates tat,...
dens und deiner Grösse, das
du in Schönheit enden, wie du
ender Antwort wird für einen
rleske: „Wirst du nicht sofort
rschel!... Ich denke gar nicht
, aber ich will gut leben."
ermittelt das tragische Ende.
Versammlung; man vermisst
gebracht. Darin verabschiedet
euenhof, dass er ihm den rechten
van Zack herein: Willi hat sich
nhofs hat ihn getötet, das Wort
rechten Zeit, das er gerade eben,
zurückgewiesen hatte.

7

Schnitzler hat sich zeitlebens mit der ?
Wortes beschäftigt, mit seiner Macht und
seiner Fähigkeit zu erhellen und zu entstellen.
viele sei hier nur *Stunde des Erkennens* dem ?
gestellt: trügerich erscheint das Wort in jener
Einakter von der Ironie des nicht wirklich
„Worte lügen" sagt Klara, als sie darauf v?
Entschluss, sich das Leben zu nehmen, ihrer
klären. Dem hier als machtlos enthüllten Wo?
serer Tragikomödie das Wort des Verantwort?
zur tödlichen Waffe wird, gegenüber.

In den Entwürfen zum *Wort* findet sich als
Vers des 18. Kapitels der Sprüche Salomons: „?
steht in der Zunge Gewalt." Das von Schnitzle?
Wort „Motto" deutet auf die Übereinstimmu?
zwischen dem biblischen Spruch und seiner Trag?
durch die Kraft seines Wortes schickte Tre?
Freund in den Tod und bewahrte sein eigenes Le?
sich dafür auch verachtete, – wenigstens in W
klar, dass wir auch im *Wort* das Werk eines Et?
wie es ja dem Kenner Schnitzlers deutlich ist,
samtes dichterisches Schaffen um zwei Pole kreist
und Ethik.

Eine ausführliche Analyse des Stückes selbst,
chen Entwürfe und des externen Materials übersch?
gezogenen Grenzen. Nur einiges sei skizzenhaft an?
besteht kein Zweifel, dass die Gestalt Treuenho?
des Dichters Peter Altenberg trägt. Dem Kenne?
Kaffeehaus- und Literatenwelt um die Jahrhu?
springen die Altenbergelemente unverkennbar i?
Anekdote beispielsweise von dem Brief an ihren
den sich das Strassenmädchen von Altenberg sch?
kann man aus dessen Werken selbst belegen.[7] Typ?
Stil Altenbergs ist die exaltierte Verehrung junger
Mädchen. Von Lisa sagt Treuenhof, sie sei „das en?

8

reinste, edelste Wesen, das es heute in dieser Stadt, ja wahrscheinlich in der ganzen Welt gibt." Die „Jünger" des Kreises reden die gleiche Sprache. Der Klavierspieler küsst einer der Dirnen die Hand und redet sie als „holdes Wesen, Gebenedeite, Süsse" an, worauf sie antwortet: „Aff! Alle reden daher wie der Treuenhof." Auch das Verhältnis von Treuenhof zu den Strassenmädchen ist Altenbergisch. „Verliebt?" sagt die kleine Tini, „Respekt haben wir vor ihm, weil er uns respektiert. Aber verliebt...," wozu man die ehrlich tieftraurigen, wenn auch orthographisch etwas unzulänglichen Zeilen zitieren könnte, die die Prostituierte Fini D. an Egon Friedell schickte, als sie vom Tode Altenbergs gehört hatte.[8]

Als der Hofrat Winkler seinen Freund Treuenhof einlädt, sich bei ihm auf dem Lande auszuruhen und den Weg zurück zur dichterischen Schöpferkraft zu finden, antwortet er: „Aufs Land – ich? Wie stellst du dir das vor? Woher soll ich die Energie für eine Reise aufbringen? Um mich in der Früh von meinem Bett bis zum Doucheapparat zu schleppen, verbrauch ich so viel Intensitäten wie ein Anderer für eine Weltumseglung." Hierzu mag man einen Brief Altenbergs an seinen Bruder Georg vom Jahre 1910 anführen:

> Meine Energielosigkeit ist bereits vollkommen pathologisch. Waschen und Anziehen sind Heldentaten der Überwindung. Wenn ich mich überwinden könnte, nach Kritzendorf zu ziehen, oder nach Baden!... Ich bin körperlich und seelisch vollkommen zerrüttet.[9]

Auch der Gedanke Treuenhofs, dass man eigentlich zum Selbstmord verpflichtet ist, wenn man seine Aufgabe in der Welt erfüllt hat, lässt sich aus Altenbergs Aufzeichnungen nachweisen: „Wandle den dir zugemessenen Weg und verschwinde!!!" Und wie Treuenhof schrieb Altenberg dann: „Vollkommene Zerstörung. Zum Selbstmord keinen Mut, also ein Leben ertragen, das unertragbar ist."[10] Freilich schrieb

Altenberg dies 1918, also 14 Jahre nachdem Schnitzler sein Altenbergdrama begonnen hatte.

Schnitzlers Beziehung zu Altenberg war etwas ambivalent. In gewissem Sinn kann man sagen, dass er ihn entdeckt hat. Altenberg erzählt es selbst, wie er im Café Central sass und eine seiner kleinen Skizzen schrieb. Da traten Schnitzler und ein paar Freunde ins Lokal, und Schnitzler sagte zu ihm: „Ich habe garnicht gewusst, dass Sie dichten!? Sie schreiben da auf Quartpapier, vor sich ein Porträt, das ist verdächtig!"[11] Wem aber diese Beschreibung zu Altenbergisch-stylisiert und deswegen biographisch zweifelhaft erscheint, der mag sich an den bisher unveröffentlichten Brief vom Jahre 1897 halten, in dem Altenberg an Schnitzler schrieb: „Sie waren der Erste, der mir über meine Manuskripte erlösende Worte sagte."[12] Wie Hofmannsthal[13] und Bahr[14] erkannte auch Schnitzler in den Prosagedichten Altenbergs den eigenen Ton eines höchst sensitiven Beobachters. Aber was Schnitzler immer hasste, war die Pose, durch die „P. A." das originelle Ich zum Original stilisierte. So schrieb er einmal von dem „nicht ganz wolkenlosen und nicht ganz echten Peter Altenberg."[15] Und je mehr Altenberg menschlich herunterkam, desto künstlicher wurde seine Affektation des „Natürlichen" und desto mehr wurde er für Schnitzler zur Verkörperung des Literaten. Vielleicht hatte er an Altenberg und *Das Wort* gedacht, als er 1912 oder 1914 sich diese Worte aufschrieb: „Ich habe nichts gegen Leute, die sich umbringen, aber ich hasse Menschen, die sich fallen lassen."[16] *Das Wort* enthält übrigens nicht nur das Porträt Altenbergs. Die Skizzen im Nachlass verraten uns, dass Schnitzler bewusst Züge von Stefan Grossmann und Alfred Polgar in den Figuren von Gleissner und Rapp und von Frau Frieda Strindberg in der Gestalt der Frau Flatterer verwendete.

Der Literat: wie hat Schnitzler den Typus gehasst, und wie liess er sich auch wieder von ihm fesseln. Sein Werk ist voll von Literaten: Biebitz im *Reigen*, Margarete und Gilbert in *Literatur*, zahlreiche Gestalten in *Der Weg ins Freie* und schliesslich ein ganzer Kreis von Gestalten im *Wort,* das man Schnitzlers Literatenstück schlechthin nennen könnte, denn Treuenhof, Frau Flatterer, Gleissner und Rapp, sie alle sind Literaten. Ihnen allen gemeinsam ist die selbstgefällige Attitüde des „Zeilenschreibers," wie Hofmannsthal den Typ einmal nannte. Von Gleissner sagt beispielsweise Rapp: „Auch das Bewusstsein seiner Unzulänglichkeit schlägt er um die Schultern wie einen Purpurmantel aus der Maskenverleihanstalt." In einer Skizze, die Schnitzler nicht mehr in die letzte Fassung des Stücks aufgenommen hat, enthüllt er Gleissners Posieren folgendermassen:

> Gleissner zu Rapp: Ich bin fort aus der Literatur. Ich lebe.
> Rapp: Du spielst zur Abwechslung einen, der lebt und aus der Literatur fort ist.

Selbstgeniesserisch spielen sie alle mit ihren Worten. Schon die grotesken Namen – Gleissner, Flatterer – charakterisieren das Scheinhaft-Oberflächliche ihres Wesens. Wie lächerlich ist beispielsweise Gleissner in seiner moralischen Selbstgerechtigkeit, mit der er die frühere Dirne zu sich „emporhebt." Er will nicht, dass sie tanzt, weil sich „das Tanzen mit dem Begriff der Keuschheit und Reinheit in keiner Weise verträgt." Er aber wird natürlich tanzen, denn er hat „keine Sünden abzuwaschen." Doch während Albine ihn wirklich liebt, versucht er, Lisa zu verführen, und da es ihm nicht gelingt, nimmt er mit, deren Schwester vorlieb.

Oder nehmen wir Frau Flatterer. Von ihr könnte man sagen, was Schnitzler einmal an Marie Reinhard schrieb: „Es gibt noch etwas unausstehlicheres als Autoren: – Autorinnen."[17] Wie lächerlich ist ihre dionysische Devise, die das Philiströse und zu Absichtliche kaum verbirgt: „Man soll sich verschwenden – überall. Ich verschwende mich immer und immer noch." Treuenhof charakterisiert sie alle, das Quartett der Literaten:

11

> Intellektuelle sind es, Weltentüftler, Literaten mit
> einem Wort. Wissen Sie, was das heisst? Sie werden
> an ihre Sargdeckel klopfen und den Totengräber
> um Papier und Bleistift bitten, um die Sensationen
> während des Begräbnisses aufzuzeichnen.

Die Verwandtschaft mit dem Einakter *Literatur* ist deutlich, in dem die schamlos narzissistische Ausbeutung der eigenen Erlebnisse für das schriftstellerische Gewerbe den Stoff zu einer köstlichen Komödie abgibt.[18]

Um einer überraschend brillianten Wendung zuliebe sind diese Literaten bereit, jederzeit ein Stück Wahrheit zu opfern. Ihre manchmal müd-lässige, dann wieder aggressiv-schlagfertige Konversation findet daher in der Sentenz, dem Aphorismus, dem Paradoxon die angemessene Form. Schnitzler liebte das Wort und den kurzen geschliffenen Spruch, – und misstraute beiden „Ein Paradoxon ist eine Lüge, die durch einen Tropfen Wahrheit vergiftet ist," sagte er.[19] Die spritzigen Paradoxa im *Wort* haben eine Ahnenreihe, die zum Frühwerk Schnitzlers zurückführt, z. B. zu dem lange ungedruckt gebliebenen Einakter von 1891, *Anatols Grössenwahn*. Dort sagt Anatol zu seinem Freund: „Hast du übrigens etwas dagegen, wenn ich das Gegenteil von dem behaupte, was ich vor einer Minute sagte?" Und Max antwortet: „Oh, ich erwarte es!"[20] Mit ganz ähnlichem Respekt vor Logik und Konsequenz widerspricht sich Treuenhof im *Wort*. Willi, behauptet er, bedürfe des Liebesglücks, um ein grosser Maler zu werden, und deshalb müsse van Zack seine Frau freigeben; einige Augenblicke später aber sagt er zu van Zack, er müsse leiden, um ganz schöpferisch zu werden. Als van Zack ihn auf diese kleine Inkonsequenz aufmerksam macht, antwortet Treuenhof, ganz der amoralische Literat: „Möglich, Widersprüche, die sind das Element, in dem wir Menschen leben können. Das Leben ist zu kurz, als dass eine Wahrheit länger existieren dürfte, als für die Dauer eines Atemzuges." Das Spiel mit Paradoxen, das in

12

der *Anatol*-Atmosphäre elegantes Geplänkel mit ernstem Unterton ist, wird im *Wort* zur Anklage gegen Unverantwortlichkeit. In der Periode, die mit Nietzsche begann und in der Generation von Schnitzler und Hofmannsthal ihren Höhepunkt fand, wurde die Fragwürdigkeit des Wortes ein zentrales literarisches, psychologisches, philosophisches und ethisches Problem. „Es ist eine schöne Narretei, das Sprechen: damit tanzt der Mensch über alle Dinge," heisst es im *Zarathustra*.[21] Doch eine zweite Parallele wird unsere Untersuchung in überraschender Weise weiterführen. In Hofmannsthal's *Brief des Lord Chandos* heisst es:

> Zuerst wurde es mir allmählich unmöglich, ein höheres oder allgemeineres Thema zu besprechen und dabei jene Worte in den Mund zu nehmen, deren sich doch alle Menschen geläufig zu bedienen pflegen. Ich empfand ein unerklärliches Unbehagen, die Worte „Geist," „Seele" oder „Körper" nur auszusprechen.[22]

Ähnlichkeiten zwischen Hofmannsthal und Schnitzler dürfen nicht erstaunen: die beiden Dichter waren fast ihr ganzes Leben lang befreundet. War auch ihre Beziehung nicht immer so nah wie zur Zeit, als der junge Loris den Prolog zum *Anatol* schrieb, so blieb sie doch immer so eng, dass auch die gereiften Dichter sich häufig ihre neuen Werke vorlasen, auch als der „Kreis" der neunziger Jahre eigentlich nicht mehr bestand. Es ist daher von grossem Interesse, dass Hofmannsthal sich den Kern des Stoffes, aus dem Schnitzler *Das Wort* gestaltete, in seinem Tagebuch notierte, und zwar im Jahre 1904, also genau zur gleichen Zeit, aus der die ersten Skizzen Schnitzlers zu diesem Drama stammen. Die nur zweiseitige Tagebucheintragung wurde bereits 1936 in der Zeitschrift *Corona* abgedruckt, doch ohne einen Hinweis auf die Verwandtschaft mit dem *Wort*, die gelegentlich zu fast wörtlichen Parallelen führt.[23] Hofmannsthals Aufzeichnung ist in einer lapidaren Sprache geschrieben, die in ihrer knappen Sachlichkeit etwas an Kleists Anekdoten erinnert. Die sonderbare Begebenheit festzuhalten, war alles, worauf es Hofmannsthal, wenigstens soweit wir Belege haben, ankam. Schnitzler aber geht es um Grundsätzliches; er stellt bloss, was ihm in der scheinhaften Atmosphäre der Literaten als unmoralisch und ekelhaft erschien: dass ein verantwortungsloser „Puppenspieler"[24] einen reinen aber schwachen Menschen in den Tod treiben kann, dass Rezensenten ihre Feder missbrauchen, um die Illusion ihrer Macht zu geniessen, dass Dandies der Literatur mit dem falschen Glanz ihrer Bonmots blüffen, dass Menschen aus der Not ihrer Undiszipliniertheit die fragwürdige Tugend eines modischen Anarchismus machen.

Den *décadents* der Literatencafés stellt Schnitzler reine Menschen gegenüber. Von Willi könnte man sagen, was Sala von dem ihm ähnlichen Felix im *Einsamen Weg* bemerkt: „Es scheint mir überhaupt, dass jetzt wieder ein besseres Geschlecht heranwächst, – mehr Haltung und weniger Geist."[25] Ebensowenig angekränkelt sind Willis Mutter und sein handfester Onkel, der Hofrat Winkler, der ja, mit dem gleichen Namen und Charakter, aus dem *Professor Bernhardi* bekannt ist.

Noch eine andere und für die Arbeitsweise Schnitzlers interessante Parallele finden wir im *Wort*. Der Klavierspieler ist derselbe Herr Nachtigall, dessen Spiel in der *Traumnovelle* die Leidenschaft der Tänzer bis zur bacchantischen Selbstvergessenheit aufpeitscht. Dort erleben wir, dass der genialisch-verschlampte Pianist maskiert in eine geheime Festlichkeit von Tänzern und Tänzerinnen geführt wird, dass er für sie spielt und dass dann, auf ein Zeichen, die Männer und Frauen ihre Kleider abwerfen und nackt weitertanzen. Im *Wort* lässt Schnitzler Nachtigall dasselbe Erlebnis auf dem Kostümfest in Lisas Gegenwart erzählen, um so ihre steigende sinnliche Erregung zu motivieren. Dass Gestalten und Szenen in Schnitzlers Phantasie so feststehen, dass sie in einem epischen ebenso gut wie in einem dramatischen Werk erscheinen

14

können, ist Beweis dafür, dass Schnitzler nicht primär Epiker oder Dramatiker war, sondern dass er Bilder, Situationen, Menschen, Gespräche, Worte in seinem schaffenden Bewusstsein trug, die dann als fertige Bausteine in diese oder jene Umgebung gerückt werden konnten.

Das Wort ist – trotz vieler interessanter Gestalten und Gedanken – etwas unglücklich angelegt. Schnitzler muss es selbst gespürt haben, sonst hätte er es wohl zu Ende geführt. Was mochte es gewessen sein, das ihn 23 Jahre lang daran hinderte, dieses Stück abzuschliessen? Mir scheint, dass es hauptsächlich zwei Schwächen hat. Einmal ist Treuenhof keine wirklich dramatische Gestalt. Das Kaffeehaus, in dem Richard Engländer die Rolle von Peter Altenberg allnächtlich vor dem Publikum seiner Jünger und Jüngerinnen spielte, diese Bühne seines Lebens sollte sich – so mochte es Schnitzler anfangs scheinen – wohl unschwer auf die dramatische Bühne übertragen lassen. Altenbergs animierte Konversation mit seinen Freunden und Claqueuren schien ja schon ein halbgeformtes Lustspiel zu sein. Soweit schien der Vorwurf bühnengerecht und mochte überdies einen besonderen Reiz für die versprechen, die das Urbild des Treuenhof schmunzelnd erkennen würden, ähnlich etwa wie die Kenner im Mynheer Peeperkorn des *Zauberberg* die kaum verhüllte Gestalt Gerhart Hauptmanns wiederfanden. Doch stellte es sich heraus, dass der etwas exaltierte Verehrer junger Mädchen, der Dichter zartpoetischer Vignetten keine dramatische, eher wohl eine epische oder lyrische Gestalt war. Das weinerliche Märtyrertum, die Neigung zum Schmarotzern, die Toulouse Lautrec-hafte Pose des Genies, das Hof hält im Kreise von Strassendirnen, – das alles ist vielleicht theaterwirksam, doch dramatisch ist es eigentlich nicht.

Aber die Problematik des Stücks geht tiefer und hängt wohl mit dem zusammen, was als ambivalent in Schnitzlers Beziehung zu Altenberg bezeichnet wurde, – und man könnte allgemeiner sagen: es hängt zusammen mit dem Schillern dieses

Typus zwischen Dichtertum und Literatentum. Diese Ambivalenz bestand ja auch objektiv in Altenberg selbst, – und er scheint sich dessen wohl bewusst gewesen zu sein. Er war ein Genie – wenn auch eines, das auf eine einzige Form des Ausdrucks beschränkt blieb – aber zugleich auch ein haltloser Neurastheniker; er war ein Mensch von kindlicher Reinheit, ein Idealist und Reformer, und zugleich eine wienerische Variante und Frühform des „Beatnik." Diese disparaten Elemente hat Schnitzler nicht in seinem Treuenhof zu vereinigen vermocht, – oder beabsichtigt. Nicht, dass er keinen echten und glaubwürdigen Dichter auf die Bühne hätte bringen können; dafür ist Filippo Loschi im *Schleier der Beatrice* ein klarer Gegenbeweis. Doch im *Wort* ist es anders: ein Kreis von Menschen betet einen Dichter als „Genie" an, der sich uns aber nie als wirklich schöpferischer Mensch, sondern allenfalls als gescheiter Aphorist darstellt. Eine Frau will eine Hilfsaktion für einen grossen Dichter von übernationalem Rang ins Werk setzen, doch sie findet nur einen übelgelaunten Hypochonder. Frau Langer spricht von dem Trost, den ihr Treuenhof beim Tode ihres Mannes gespendet hat, doch wir sehen nur einen Egoisten, einen literarischen Narziss, doch keinen echten Freund. Man fragt sich, wie Treuenhof einen solchen Einfluss ausüben kann, dass sich ein junger Mensch wegen eines hingeworfenen Wortes dieses Mannes das Leben nimmt. Man versteht es nicht, weil Treuenhof zu klein und karikiert geraten ist, weil er weit hinter Peter Altenberg zurückbleibt. Dadurch bekommt das ganze Stück etwas Unglaubwürdiges.

Warum ist es aber dazu gekommen? Mir scheint, die Gestalt des Treuenhof ist das Ergebnis zweier nicht ganz zur Harmonie geratener Intentionen Schnitzlers. Einmal wollte er das Porträt eines Dichters geben mit all dem Genialen und auch Charlatanhaften, all dem Feingefühl und der Selbstsucht, die dem Original im Café Central eigen waren. Andererseits hatte er einen „Vorfall," der die Oberflächlichkeit des Literaten blosslegte. Und wie so oft bei Schnitzler wurde das Ethische

16

schliesslich die Hauptsache. Welches Problem aber könnte mehr im Mittelpunkt aller Ethik stehen als das der menschlichen Verantwortlichkeit? Um die Unverantwortlichkeit, die im Missbrauch des Wortes liegt, überzeugend darzustellen, musste Schnitzler seinem Treuenhof einen grossen Teil seiner Sympathie entziehen; so wurde er immer mehr zum Literaten, bis man ihm schliesslich weder Genie noch menschliche Wärme zu glauben vermag. In einer kurzen Bemerkung Schnitzlers (wahrscheinlich aus den Jahren 1906-07) sehe man eine Andeutung, dass der Dichter selbst die Schwäche in der Gestalt Treuenhofs ähnlich gesehen hat; er schrieb dort: „Treuenhof nicht nur lächerlich, sondern doch auch ergreifend." Doch auch in der zwanzig Jahre später geschriebenen Fassung ist Schnitzler das erste besser gelungen als das letztere, denn ergreifend ist ja nur die Gestalt Willi Langers geworden, des Opfers des missbrauchten Wortes, des reinen Toren.

Wir haben also in diesem wichtigen Werk aus Schnitzlers Nachlass eine Tragikomödie, deren zentrales Problem die Frage der Verantwortung ist, die der Gebrauch der Sprache dem Menschen auferlegt. Treuenhof folgt gewissermassen der Devise „vivat verbum, pereat homo." Die Positionen des Literaten und des Ethikers sind vielleicht nirgends klarer in diesem Stück formuliert als in den zwei Sätzen Treuenhofs und Winklers, welcher hier zweifellos für Schnitzler selbst spricht. Als Treuenhof merkt, was er angerichtet hat, sagt er : „Worte sind nichts," und Winkler erwidert ihm: „Worte sind alles. Wir haben ja nichts anderes." Wir: das heisst wir als Menschen und wir als Dichter. Und Schnitzler erweiterte diesen Gedanken in einer Notiz zu diesem Drama, die mir seine philosophische und ethische Absicht zusammenzufassen scheint:

> Zum 'Wort.' Unsere ganze Moral besteht vielleicht
> nur darin, aus diesem unpräzisen Material, das uns
> das Lügen so leicht, so verantwortungslos, so ent-

schuldbar macht, aus der Sprache etwas Besseres
zu machen. Mit Worten so wenig zu lügen als
möglich ist.

ANMERKUNGEN

[1] Der bisher unveröffentlichte Brief Schnitzlers an Alfred Kerr vom
5. Juli 1918 befindet sich in Abschrift in Schnitzlers Nachlass.

[2] Schnitzler war bekanntlich ein unermüdlicher Verbesserer seiner
Entwürfe. So schrieb er z. B. über die Arbeit an der *Komödie der
Verführung* an Werner Hegemann am 18. Oktober 1927, dass er „die
Szenen zwischen Aurelie und Falkenir sowohl im ersten wie im
dritten Akt buchstäblich 40 – 50 Mal geschrieben und diktiert habe".

[3] Am 7. August 1904 trug Schnitzler, anlässlich eines Zusammenseins
mit Bahr, das folgende in sein Tagebuch ein: „Über Altenberg.
Seine 'Freunde' veranstalten eine Versammlung, wie ihm zu helfen
sei (Krankheit, Noth) – er selbst wohnt bei. Plötzlich, nach verschiedenen Reden steht Frau Loos, früheres Frl. Obertimpfler,
hübsche Schauspielerin auf und sagt: ...Man soll ihm gar nicht
helfen... Es ist schön, wenn solche Leute jung sterben... u.s.w. Da
ergrimmt Peter Altenberg und schreit – 'Ich will aber nicht sterben,
ich will leben...' (Kostbare Scene für das 'Literatenstück') –"
Weitere Tagebucheinträge vom 5. Februar und 27. März 1905 weisen
auf die Beschäftigung mit dem Stoff hin, und am 11. Januar 1906 be-
richtet das Tagebuch von einem Zusammensein Schnitzlers mit Felix
Salten: „Über Frau Marie Lang, deren Sohn sich wegen Frau Loos
umgebracht (Altenberg: Stirb... Sie ist eine Göttin) und die Herrn
Stefan Gr. für einen reinen Menschen hält. (Das Stück ist seit
Monaten scenirt, unter 'P.A.'). –" (Gr. ist Schnitzlers Abkürzung für
Grossmann.) Für die hier zitierten Stellen aus dem Tagebuch, wie
für manche anderen Hinweise und jahrelange Hilfe bin ich dem Sohn
des Dichters, Herrn Heinrich Schnitzler, zu grösstem Dank verpflichtet.

[4] Vgl. die Briefe Schnitzlers an Otto Brahm vom 12. und 28. Juli und
vom 6. August 1906 in *Der Briefwechsel Arthur Schnitzler – Otto
Brahm*, herausgegeben und eingeleitet von Oskar Seidlin, Berlin
1953, pp. 189-195.
Der Titel des Stückes stand auch nicht immer fest. In einer Skizze vom
Jahre 1906 heisst es *Unser aller Herr, das Wort*; in einem Entwurf
vom Frühjahr 1907 wird der Titel *Der Hexenkessel* erwogen.

[5] In einer anderen Skizze (wahrscheinlich vom Jahre 1905) schrieb

Schnitzler von Frau Flatterer, sie „fühlt sich als Sphinx, sie ist etwa vierzig Jahre und ihr Rätsel ist noch immer nicht gelöst worden."

[6] In einem Entwurf hat Schnitzler Lisa folgendermassen charakterisiert: „Frau Zack ist ein hübsches, puppenhaftes, mit modernen, unverstandenen Ideen vollgepropftes Wesen, zwischen absichtlicher Dämonie und Süssigkeit hin- und herschwankend."

[7] „DER 'KOBERER' (KUPPLER)
'Du', sagte der Graf zur Mitzi G., 'wer hat dir denn diesen Brief an mich aufgesetzt?!'
'Aufgesetzt?! Aufgesetzt?! Wie meinen Sie das?!'
'Aufgesetzt! Selbstverständlich hast du den nicht selbst verfasst!'
'Weshalb nicht?! Bin ich denn gar so dumm?!'
'Nein, ja. Aber diesen Brief hast *du* einmal *nicht* verfasst!'
'Wer sollte ihn denn verfasst haben?!'
,Das weiss ich nicht. Das weisst nur *du*. Du, Mitzerl, ich gebe dir 100 Kronen, wenn du mir den Namen nennst!'
,100 Kronen?! Gib mir 150?'
,Also 150!'
,*Der Peter*!'
,Was für ein Peter?!'
,No, der Peter, der Peter Altenberg!' . . ."
Ernst Randak, *Peter Altenberg oder das Genie ohne Fähigkeiten*, Graz und Wien, 1961, pp. 117-119.

[8] *Das Altenbergbuch*, hg. von Egon Friedell, Leipzig, 1921, pp. 389f.

[9] *Ib.*, p. 49

[10] *Ib.*, p. 371.

[11] „So wurde ich," in Peter Altenberg, *Das Glück der verlorenen Stunden*, München, o. J., p. 310 f.

[12] Die Briefe Altenbergs an Schnitzler befinden sich in dessen Nachlass. Da die Beziehung der beiden Dichter bisher weitgehend unbekannt geblieben ist, seien hier einige Stellen aus Altenbergs Briefen an Schnitzler angeführt. Nach ziemlich formell gehaltenen Schreiben vom Mai 1893 und Juli 1894 folgte aus Gmünden am 30. Juli 1895 ein weit persönlicher gehaltener Brief, in dem Altenberg u.a. schrieb:

„Kommen Sie doch herüber. Sie sind gesund und mobil. Kommen Sie mit Richard Beer-Hofmann. Ich bin wie stets von Gmünden tief entzückt. Es ist gleichsam für mich geschaffen. Und dann, es muss mir halt die Welten-Schönheit repräsentieren. Wenn die Leute am Strande hin u. hertrippeln, ist es Ostende, Scheveningen, wenn die Musik spielt und Damen in Chiné-Seide erscheinen, ist es Karlsbad, Marienbad, wenn der Traunstein ziegelroth wird, ist es die Schweiz

u. wenn der Abendfriede kommt, so ist es die Welt, die Zukunft, das Ende. Glauben Sie mir, lieber Dr. Arthur, wir Armen sind wie gewisse Kranke. Gewisse Organe verfeinern sich, erhöhen ihre Leistungsfähigkeiten, um den Ausfall anderer zu decken. So ist es mit der Potenz in jeder Form. Ekonomische(*sic*) Kräfte, sexuelle Kräfte, werden durch erhöhte seelische ausgeglichen. Das Gehirn übernimmt gleichsam ihre Aufgabe und macht sich die Verkümmerung zu Nutze. Sie werden sagen: ,Das ist nicht Harmonie, mein Lieber…' Wenn sie das aber nicht antworten, werde ich Sie noch höher schätzen, nach meinem berühmten!? Ausspruch: ,*Weise sein heisst, auch das noch verstehen, was man nicht mehr versteht*!!' Adieu, also kommen Sie doch herüber.

Ihr aufrichtig freundschaftlicher
Richard Engländer."

Im Jahre 1897 schrieb Altenberg den folgenden Brief:

„Lieber Dr. Arthur Schnitzler:
Sie können sich garnicht vorstellen, wie tief mich ihre (*sic*) wunderbare Aufmerksamkeit ergriffen hat.
Sie haben einen Bankrottirer des Lebens zu seinen sparsamen Augenblicken des Glückes einen heiligen Augenblick hinzugefügt. Mögen Sie, edler Sieger im Leben, nicht sich wundern, wenn Einer, der durch körperliche, seelische und ökonomische Leiden besiegt und zerdrückt ist, manchesmal mit Verwunderung auf Jene blickt, welchen das Schicksal freundlicher lächelt. Mögen Sie mir es verzeihen, der ich die ,*ewige Bewegung*,' das ,*innere Stürmen*' für das Schönste halte, wenn ich mit Verwunderung auf ihren (*sic*) innigeren Freundeskreis blicke, in welchem uralte Greise wie Leo Ebermann und Gustav Schwarzkopf Stammsitze haben.
Merkwürdig, Sie waren der Erste, der mir über meine Manuskripte erlösende Worte sagte. Nun bringen Sie mir ein wundervolles Urtheil von G. Hauptmann.
Sie haben mich (*sic*) imer (*sic*) fein und zart gegen mich benommen.
Möge in kommender Zeit ein freundschaftliches Zusammenleben mir Gelegenheit geben, meine keimenden Neigungen auswachsen zu lassen. Das wünsche ich mir!
Schreiben Sie mir aus Berlin. Sie erleben dort gewiss sehr viel.
Ich selbst lebe in Sehnsucht nach meiner schwarzen Freundin *Nahbadûh*, diesem ,letzten Wahnsinn meiner Seele!'

Ihr
Peter Altenberg."

20

Im Jahre 1909 schrieb Altenberg wie folgt an Schnitzler:

„Wenn Sie mein zerfahrenes unruhiges verkommenes Leben auch nur annähernd kennen könnten, würden Sie sich nicht wundern, dass ich Ihnen erst heute für Ihr wunderbares Schreiben danke. Ich kann es ruhig sagen, ich bin, bei meinem eng umgrenzten Talentchen, voll und ganz gewürdigt worden, also eigentlich ein besonderes Gnadengeschenk des in anderen Angelegenheiten heimtückischen Schicksals!
Mit herzlichstem Grusse an Ihre edle Frau..."

Altenberg lebte weitgehend von der Unterstützung seiner Freunde. 1904 erliess Alfred Kerr unter dem Namen Jean Pauls einen Aufruf „An die Lebenden," worin er zu einer Sammlung für Altenberg aufforderte; doch, in Kerrs eigenen Worten, „das Ergebnis waren ein paar tausend Mark... Vier Jahre danach regte der Dichter selbst eine neue Sammlung an... (Leider kam nichts Nennenswertes heraus)." (*Das Altenbergbuch, op. cit.*, pp. 93 ff.) Altenberg schrieb damals an Kerr: „Vielleicht könnte Deutschland meiner Vaterstadt beweisen, dass ich ein unterstützungswerter Schriftsteller sei?" Aus dieser Stelle ersehen wir, dass der im *Wort* entwickelte Einfall, die Unterstützung Treuenhofs von Deutschland ausgehen zu lassen, auch ein Stück Altenbergbiographie ist.

Dass auch Schnitzler Altenberg geldlich unterstützt hat, ergibt sich aus dem folgenden Brief und Telegramm. Vom Hotel Panhans auf dem Semmering schrieb Altenberg am 7. November 1912:

„Lieber Dr. Arthur Schnitzler,
ich schreibe es Ihnen ganz klip (*sic*) und klar, denn alles Andere hätte gar keinen Sinn: Eine Reihe von Menschen, die mich *bisher* durch *fixe monatliche Beiträge* unterstützt haben, sind allmälig (*sic*) ‚ausgesprungen.' Ich frage daher bei Ihnen, dem vom Schicksale Begünstigten, an, ob Sie oder Andere (Beer-Hoffmann (*sic*), Hugo Hofmannsthal, Hermann Bahr etc. etc.) mir die Sorge meines Lebensabends (‚tiefste Lebensnacht' sollte es eigentlich lauten) erleichtern wollen!?!? Bis zum 53. Jahre habe ich mich so ‚*durchgefrettet*'. Ich bin seit 8 Wochen von einer ‚allgemeinen Nervenentzündung' (polyneuritis) Tag und Nacht *gefoltert*, dazu die seelische Depression!
Ich bitte sehr, dieses Schreiben als *Geheimnis* zu betrachten.
Ich appellire (*sic*) an den Menschen *und* den Dichter. Meine Tage sind gerichtet *und* gezählt, da gibt es keine Demütigung mehr, man

ist schon halb wo anders, dort wo die Beurteilungen des Menschen und seiner Seele *anders* gewertet werden.

Ihr unseliger
Peter Altenberg

Es ist ein Notschrei eines schwerst Bedrängten. Geheimnis!!!"

Aus Altenbergs Telegramm geht hervor, dass Schnitzler ihm damals half: „Unter heissen tränen meinen dank kann nicht schreiben es wird nicht mehr lang dauern ihr unglücklicher Altenberg."

Altenberg musste sich damals auf dem Semmering einer Kur unterziehen, die ihn von seinem Alkoholismus heilen sollte. Der tief unter seiner Abhängigkeit leidende Dichter verdächtigte gelegentlich seinen Bruder, dass er ihn unnötiger Weise im Sanatorium der Freiheit beraube. Im April 1913 schrieb er wieder an Schnitzler:

„Lieber lieber Herr Dr. Arthur Schnitzler,
ein Verlorener, Zusammengestürzter, unmittelbar nach einem paradiesischen Semmering-Jahr 1912, ein *tiefst* Verzweifelter, wendet sich an Sie als Menschenfreundlichen und Dichter vor allem, dann als Kollegen und langjährigen litterarischen Genossen... Hilfe, Rettung, Erbarmen, in einer so *schauerlichen* Situation, die noch nie, noch nie, noch nie, ein Dichter, ein Künstler-Mensch erlitten hat! Der süssen unentbehrlichen Freiheit beraubt, verbringe ich meine Tage und Nächte in unermesslichen Qualen, eingefangen, kontrollirt wie ein *böses, gefährliches, giftiges Reptil!*
Hilfe, Errettung, Weg ins Freie!
Auch geht es mir ökonomisch schlecht, und bitte ich Sie und Hofmannsthal um die mir zugesagten 20 kr. monatlich seit *November* 1912, da ich gerade damals zusammenbrach und nicht mehr danken konnte! *Hilfe*, um Gotteswillen, ehe ich ganz zerstört bin!
Ich möchte auf dem Semmering ruhig vegetiren (*sic*), in Freiheit und Frieden! Hilfe von *Bruder*-Seelen! Dichter, Künstler, Menschen, helft mir!!!

Peter Altenberg"

Als ärztlicher Berater war Schnitzler damals auch mit Altenbergs Bruder in Verbindung: nicht alle Briefe sind uns erhalten, doch der folgende vom 22. April 1913 befindet sich in Abschrift unter Schnitzlers Papieren:

„Lieber Peter Altenberg.
Gestern habe ich also Ihren Bruder gesprochen und ihm erklärt, dass Sie meiner Überzeugung nach die Anstalt gerade so gut noch in dieser Woche als später verlassen könnten, da ja die Möglichkeit,

22

dass Sie sich in vollkommener Freiheit dem Alkohol wieder allzu sehr ergeben, in drei oder vier Wochen keine wesentlich geringere sein dürfte als heute oder morgen. Er scheint nun auch durchaus geneigt, Sie schon in wenigen Tagen aus dem Sanatorium zu nehmen, möchte aber gern, was auch ich sehr vernünftig finde, dass Sie wenigstens die erste Zeit auf dem Semmering noch nicht in einem Hotel, sondern eventuell im Kurhaus bei Dr. Hansy zubrächten. Sollte das aber nicht durchführbar sein, so wäre er wohl auch mit dem Vorschlag einverstanden, den Sie mir selbst gemacht haben: für die ersten Tage den Ihnen sympathischen Wärter auf den Semmering mitzunehmen, so dass doch ein gewisser Übergang, der auch Ihren jetzigen Ärzten wünschenswert erscheinen dürfte, von der Anstaltsbehandlung zum Leben in vollkommerer Freiheit geschaffen würde.

Ihr Bruder ist es nun einmal, der die volle Verantwortung für Sie übernehmen muss. In seinem Interesse liegt es gewiss nicht, dass Sie noch länger in der Anstalt verbleiben; wenn nun gewisse eher formelle Forderungen noch erfüllt werden müssen, so verlieren Sie doch darüber nicht die Geduld; es handelt sich bestimmt nur mehr um wenige Tage. Brauchen Sie noch weiter hin meine Intervention eventuell bei Herrn Primarius Richter, so stehe ich Ihnen ganz zur Verfügung.

Mit herzlichem Gruss Ihr
Arthur Schnitzler."

[13] Hugo von Hofmannsthal, „Das Buch von Peter Altenberg," *Die Zukunft*, 5. November 1896 (und in *Die Berührung der Sphären*, Berlin 1931, pp. 87-95).

[14] Hermann Bahr, „Ein neuer Dichter" in *Renaissance*, Berlin 1897, pp. 45-52.

[15] Brief Schnitzlers an Otto Brahm vom 3. Juni 1898, in *Der Briefwechsel Arthur Schnitzler – Otto Brahm, op. cit.*, p. 76.

[16] Mappe 6 des Nachlasses.

[17] Brief vom 8. Juli 1895 aus Karlsbad (im Nachlass).

[18] Den Literaten als schnoddrigen „Kritiker" klassischer Dichtung verkörpert Rapp, der sich – in einer später nicht benutzten Skizze zum *Wort* – über den *Faust* äussern sollte:
„Wie sich der Autor das Leben vorstellt. Ein Kneiplokal und das Bettchen eines geilen Bürgermädchens. Warum die junge Dame ihre Mutter vergiften muss unerfindlich. Technische Hilflosigkeit. Weshalb bestellt sie der Ritter nicht in seine Wohnung?"

[19] Mappe 7 des Nachlasses.

[20] Athur Schnitzler, *Meisterdramen*, Frankfurt a.M., 1955, p. 588.

[21] Friedrich Nietzsche, *Also sprach Zarathustra*, III, „Der Genesende".

[22] Hugo von Hofmannsthal, *Gesammelte Werke*, Berlin 1934, 3. Band, 2. Teil, pp. 193f.

[23] „Rodaun, 30. IX. (1904) – Zwei Vorfälle aus dem ‚Seelen' kreise, der um den Dichter N. gruppiert ist." In: „Aus Hugo von Hofmannsthal Tagebüchern," *Corona*, Sechstes Jahr (1936), Fünftes Heft, pp. 572f. – In der Fassung der Gesamtausgabe – Hugo von Hofmannsthal, *Aufzeichnungen*, Frankfurt am Main 1959, pp. 135f. – wird der „Dichter" statt N. Peter Altenberg genannt, womit Herbert Steiner, der Herausgeber, zweifellos den authentischen Text wiederhergestellt hat. – Als Beispiel der Parallele sei die Stelle zitiert, die der Rede Lisas auf Seite 7 dieser Arbeit entspricht. Bei Hofmannsthal sagt sie:
„ ‚Ich liebe N. mehr als ihr alle, ich liebe seine Seele und die Gebärden seiner Seele. Und ich weiss nichts Schöneres, als ihn so sterben zu sehen, in einem Winkel, mit einer dürftigen Decke zugedeckt. O rührt nicht an das Wunder des Sterbens. Pauvre Lélian? wer wollte ihn um die Schönheit seines Endes bringen?' – Da schnellt N. wütend aus seinem Fauteuil auf: ‚Dumme Gans,' schreit er sie an, ‚verfluchte dumme Gans! ich will nicht sterben! ich will leben! ich will ein warmes Zimmer und einen Gasofen, einen amerikanischen Schaukelstuhl, eine Rente, Orangen, Jam, Kraftsuppe, Filets Mignon; ich will leben!' "

[24] Der Mensch, der mit Menschen spielt, kommt bei Schnitzler öfters vor: Georg Merklin im *Puppenspieler* und Treuenhof haben manche Ähnlichkeiten: beide sind Dichter, Unbehauste, die Bindung und Bürgerlichkeit ablehnen, die im Spiel mit Menschen zwar eine vorübergehende Befriedigung finden, aber letztlich doch die um das Leben Geprellten sind.

[25] Arthur Schnitzler, *Die Theaterstücke*, Berlin 1922, 3. Band, p. 102.

SCHNITZLER IN FRANZÖSISCHER SICHT

Von Joseph H. Dayag

„Unter den modernen deutschen Autoren hat Schnitzler die meiste Verwandtschaft mit den Franzosen. In ihm kommen französischer Esprit und deutsche Skepsis zu einem angenehmen Ausgleich,"[1] schreibt Josef Karl Ratislav 1911 und sagt später in der selben Studie: „Die Liebelei hat Schnitzlers Ruhm begründet. Das Drama steht in einer literarischen Tradition, die an Dumas' Kameliendame anknüpft."[2] Heinz Kindermann in seinem *Wegweiser durch die moderne Literatur in Österreich*[3] und Josef Nadler in seiner *Literaturgeschichte Österreichs*[4] weisen, nebst anderen Autoren, auf den Einfluss hin, den Gustave Flaubert und Guy de Maupassant auf Schnitzler ausgeübt haben. Und Leo Feigl meint in *Arthur Schnitzler und Wien*,[5] dass Schnitzler in seinen ersten Werken „tief im Naturalismus" wurzelt. „Die Schule Zolas," sagt er, „ist in seinen ersten Werken leicht zu erkennen." Zusammenfassend erklärt Kurt Bergel in der Einleitung zu dem von ihm herausgegebenen Briefwechsel zwischen Georg Brandes und Arthur Schnizler:[6] „Die engen kulturellen Beziehungen zwischen Österreich und Frankreich sind bekannt. Die Biographen Schnitzlers vermuten einen Einfluss des französischen Gesellschaftsstückes auf seine Erstlingswerke, ohne dass sie diesen Einfluss bisher wissenschaftlich nachgewiesen hätten. Immerhin hat Schnitzler selbst gesprächsweise solche Einflüsse, ohne sie näher zu bezeichnen, zugegeben. Jedenfalls fällt eine Ähnlichkeit im Charakter und in der Technik des Gespräches bei Gyp* (*Autour du Mariage*), Monnier (*Scènes populaires*) und Schnitzler (*Anatol*) auf, und man wird wohl sagen dürfen, dass der französische Einfluss für ... Schnitzlers Jugendschriften, wenn auch nicht für ... (seine) Reifewerke wichtig war."[7] Wir müssen hier wohl hinzufügen, dass Schnitzler in einem Briefe an Brandes, datiert vom 11. Juni 1901,[8] in Bezug auf *Leutnant Gustl* (womit er den „inneren Monolog" in die deutsche Literatur eingeführt hat) wörtlich schreibt: „Mir aber wurde der erste Anlass zu der Form durch eine Geschichte von Dujardin gegeben, betitelt 'les lauriers sont coupés'." Schnitzler war einige Male in Paris und soll auch durch Jeanne Marni,** mit der er in persönlichem und schriftlichem Verkehr stand, hinsichtlich *Anatol* und *Reigen* beeinflusst worden sein.[9]. Wie wir aus einem Artikel Marcel Dunants vom Jahre 1932 in der *Revue d'Allemagne*,[10] betitelt „Arthur Schnitzler et la France" (leider wird der Inhalt dem Titel nicht gerecht), erfahren, war Schnitzler mit einer Anzahl angesehener französischer Schriftsteller persönlich bekannt. Dunant nennt uns Claude Anet, die Colette, Lucie Delarue-Mardrus, Claude Farrère, Paul Géraldy, Jean Giradoux und Paul Morand. All dies und auch Gründe allgemeiner Natur sollten uns dazu bringen der Meinung der so literaturfreudigen Franzosen über Arthur Schnitzler nachzugehen, zumal ja auch ein nicht ganz unbeträchtlicher Teil von Schnitzlers Schaffen ins Französische übersetzt worden ist.***

Ein geistreiches französisches Wort sagt: „L'étranger, c'est la postérité contemporaine." Der Bestand künstlerischen

* Marie-Antoinette de Riquetti de Mirabeau, comtesse de Martel de Janville, 1850-1932.
** Jeanne-Mancel de Grandfort, 1854-1910.
*** Siehe das am Ende folgende Verzeichnis.

Schaffens zeigt sich erst in der Distanz, von der aus die Beschauer die gemässe Perspektive gewinnen können für die Beurteilung des Werkes. Die Nachwelt hat die zeitliche Entfernung hierfür, sie ist unbeeinflusst von dem, was man den „literarischen Strassenlärm" nennen könnte. Keine verwirrenden Begleitumstände trüben mehr die Aufnahmsbereitschaft des Publikums. Umriss und Inhalt bieten sich unverbrämt dem Urteil dar. Der zeitgenössische Ausländer hat statt des zeitlichen den intellektuellen Abstand. Als Aussenstehender findet er oft eher den Blickwinkel, der ihm die passende Einsicht in das Werk gewährt.

Wir müssen aber feststellen, dass, *mirabile dictu*, bis dato, zumindest unseres Wissens nach, die Behandlung dieses Themas, wie in unserem Titel gestellt, vernachlässigt worden ist. Bergel, z.B., der den vorher erwähnten Briefwechsel ausserordentlich gründlich eingeleitet und kommentiert hat, gibt dort selbst im Anhang ein Verzeichnis der Schriften über Arthur Schnitzler, dass sechzig Titel anführt – dreiunddreissig aus dem deutschen, siebenundzwanzig aus dem englischen und nicht ein einziger aus dem französischen Sprachbereiche stammend, obwohl er französische Quellen in anderen Zusammenhängen zitiert. Gewiss, wir können nicht umhin, zuzugeben, dass aus mancherlei Gründen es naheliegt, dass die literarische Persönlichkeit Arthur Schnitzlers im französischen Kulturbereiche weniger Aufmerksamkeit gefunden hat als im angelsächsischen. Immerhin hat er aber eine gewisse Aufmerksamkeit gefunden und es lohnt sich der Natur dieser Aufmerksamkeit gewahr zu werden.

Leider muss es uns versagt bleiben, im Rahmen dieser wenigen Worte auch nur annähernd dieser Aufgabe gerecht zu werden. Die Erfassung des gesamten Materials muss wohl einer Reise nach dem Ort der Quellen vorbehalten bleiben; eine eingehende Beschäftigung mit unserem Gegenstande mag auch die

27

Möglichkeit der Einbeziehung anderer lateinsprachiger Länder mit Eröffnung neuer Aspekte ergeben. Hier wollen wir zunächst versuchen, festzustellen, in welche Hauptkategorien die allgemeine Meinung über Schnitzler zerlegt werden kann und dann anhand einiger weniger bezeichnender französischer Quellen sehen, wie weit sich die französischen Meinungen mit den anderen decken.

Hören wir zunächst, was Selma Koehler 1923 in einem Artikel betitelt: „The question of moral responsibility in the dramatic works of Arthur Schnitzler"[11] zu sagen hat: „... the ethical worth of Schnitzler's writings can scarcely be over-estimated ... Especially is this true of his earlier dramatic works. In his later plays the moral impact is more subtle and implied." Und dann zitiert die Verfasserin aus der *North American Review*:[12] „... this 'cynicism' proceeds not from a distrust in human nature, but from an extraordinary astute perception of its frailties – the legacy of all physicians of the human body."

F. W. Kaufmann schreibt 1933 in einem Artikel, „Zur Frage der Wertung in Schnitzlers Werk:"[13] „Als Hauptcharakterzug des Impressionismus gilt fast unbestritten, dass er im wesentlichen Oberflächenkunst sei, dass er spiegele, ohne Wertungen zu versuchen, dass er die Unterscheidung von Gut und Schlecht grundsätzlich unterdrücke. Namentlich der Wiener Impressionismus streite dem Menschen alles höher gestimmte Fühlen ab und führe sein ganzes Handeln auf niedrigste Triebe zurück; das sei zum wenigsten der Gesamteindruck. Für Schnitzler wird in diesem Sinne noch erschwerend sein psychoanalytisches Interesse und eine verborgene Erotik in die Wagschale geworfen. Als das Wesentliche an seinem Werke erscheint dann die Flucht vor Desillusionen, Alltag, Tod und Verfall, das Suchen nach einem letzten Rausch in Schönheit und Glück in einer unglaublichen Leichtfertigkeit in der Auffassung ehelicher Verpflichtung. Damit wird der Impressionismus recht

28

einseitig zu einem schwelgerischen Sich-zu-Tode-Blühen der bürgerlichen Kunst."

Hier haben wir bereits die beiden Hauptkategorien in der Beurteilung der literarischen Persönlichkeit Schnitzlers. Auf die knappste Formel gebracht ist er für die einen das Symbol der Dekadenz des *fin de siècle* und für die anderen vergegenwärtigt er den berühmten Spruch des wiener Professor Nothnagel, dass nur ein guter Mensch ein guter Arzt sein könne. Und dieser gute Arzt Schnitzler erkennt die menschliche Natur und versteht sie.

1908 schreibt Maurice Muret in *La Nouvelle Revue*[14] eine Studie über Schnitzler, die er „Un parisien de Vienne" nennt. Er meint dort, dass alle drei Wiener (Bahr, Hofmannsthal, Schnitzler) ein wenig der Tiefe mangeln, „ils ont le souffle un peu court." Weit davon entfernt die Menschheit in ihrer Gesamtheit darzustellen, das Leben in seiner Fülle, kultivieren sie nur ein enges Gebiet, die Gefühle, die sie zeichnen, sind recht wenig komplex und nur wenig tief. Aber bei den besten unter den Wiener Poeten, ganz besonders bei Arthur Schnitzler „quelle grâce captivante, quel charme exquis et leger!" Obwohl Muret Schnitzler den Erzähler dem Dramatiker Schnitzler vorzieht, versteht er des letzteren Erfolge und erzählt von dem begeisterten Feuilleton, dass Emile Faguet* nach der Lektüre einer Manuskriptübersetzung von *Liebelei* im *Journal des Débats* veröffentlichte und wo er erklärte, dass „ce chef-d'oeuvre scénique était une chose remarquablement vigoureuse et directe." Muret wendet sich energisch gegen einen zu nahen Vergleich von Maupassant und Schnitzler. Schnitzler sei weich und Maupassant hart. Im Aufbau, im Stil, in der Form seien sie ebenso verschieden wie in ihrer inneren Stellungnahme. Wie alle Realisten der französischen Feder, malt Maupassant mehr als er erzählt. Er lässt seine Charaktere sich durch ihre Handlungen äussern und durch ihre wunderbar

---

* 1847-1916; seit 1896 am *J. des D.* Nachfolger des berühmten Lemaître als Literaturkritiker.

knappen Dialoge. Er greift kaum in seine Geschichten ein. Schnitzler mache das ganz anders. Vielmals auf indirekte Weise würden uns die Umstände durch Gespräche und Bemerkungen dritter enthüllt. Murat versteht nicht, warum die Deutschen auf der literarischen Verwandtschaft zwischen Maupassant und Schnitzler bestünden, aber er gibt zu, die Geschichten Schnitzlers hätten „un certain air de chez nous... Ces contes aimables et vifs, tant pleins de clarté, de fine malice de mélancolie élégante, d'une ironie tempérée de sentiment ou sentimentalité tempérée d'ironie, relèvent de la tradition française et latine bien plus que de la tradition allemande." Der Deutsche bewege sich nur unbehaglich, meint Muret, in einem Raume, der ihm knapp zugemessen sei. Er würde mittelmässig, wenn der Brauch eines literarischen Genre ihn daran hindere, alles zu sagen und alles völlig zu sagen. Der Dekamerone des Boccaccio, die Fabeln des La Fontaine seien lateinische Meisterwerke. Schnitzlers Erzählungen, sosehr sie auch einen germanischen Stempel tragen mögen, gehören zu der selben Familie. Zwischen den französischen und den deutschen Erzählern bilde Schnitzler eine Art Zwischenglied „moins reproché, certes, malgré l'identité de l'idiome – du type allemand d'Allemagne que du type français." Und immer wieder kommt Muret (der übrigens geborener Welschschweizer war) darauf zurück wie französisch, ja pariserisch Schnitzler wäre und dass sein Mangel an Tiefe weit überschattet würde von seiner Anmut.

André Tibal stösst 1909 in der *Revue de Paris*[15] in ein ähnlich klingendes Horn. Auch er beschreibt wie Muret auf fast zwanzig Seiten einige Werke Schnitzlers, wobei er z.B. vom Inhalt des *Weg ins Freie* nichts als die zwischen Georg v. Wergenthin und Anna spielende Geschichte zu erzählen weiss. Er hat viel Lob für Schnitzler (und andere Wiener), er bewundert die Finesse und Delikatesse, die Schnitzler in allen literarischen Situationen zu bewahren weiss. Er preist das Aristokratische in Schnitzlers Talent, aber er sieht ihn als einen Dekadenten und meint, Schnitzlers Auffassung von der Liebe sei: „L'amour n'est qu'une sympathie d'épidermes, les âmes ne se connaissent, jamais." Und das Morbide triumphiere über das Vitale.

Auch Léon Pineau spielt in seiner *L'évolution du roman en Allemagne au XIXe siècle*[16] den Österreicher Schnitzler gegen die Deutschen aus. Die Novelle, meint er, hätte eine natürliche Tendenz die Dialogform anzunehmen. Auch in Deutschland, aber in Wien hätte die Novelle in Zwiegesprächform ihren besten Repräsentanten gefunden. In Wien mit seinen Salons, wo man sich unterhält, mit seinen Literatenkaffeehäusern, mit seinen leichten und geistreichen Feuilletons, mit einem volkstümlichen Theater in natürlicher und wirklichkeitsnaher Sprache. Und er nennt den Anatol: „une des oeuvres les plus originales de la littérature allemande contemporaine."

Félix Bertaux, der auch ein Vorwort zu einem der übersetzten Werke Schnitzlers schrieb, meint 1928 in *Panorama de la littérature allemande contemporaine*,[17] dass die Erotik das Leitmotif Schnitzlers wäre, eine Erotik verschieden von der philosophischen Auffassung der Deutschen, wo, z.B. bei Dehmel, eine Verschmelzung des Sinnlichen und des Metaphysischen angestrebt würde. Don Juan hat hier seinen tragischen Elan verloren, aber die unwiderrufliche Traurigkeit, hervorgerufen durch den Verlust der Illusion, beherrscht den Menschen.

Geneviève Bianquis (die ihre Doktorarbeit über österreichische Poesie schrieb) in ihrer *Histoire de la littérature allemande*,[18] Nicolas Ségur in seiner *Histoire de la littérature européenne*[19] und noch so manche andere, sie alle anerkennen Schnitzlers überragendes Talent, aber sie alle sehen ihn als den dekadenten Exponenten einer morbiden, leichtlebigen Gesellschaft. Erst in einem neueren Werke, 1959, finden wir Anzeichen einer gewissen Wendung. Claude David, Professor an der Sorbonne, schreibt in *L'époque Bismarckienne et L'Allemange contem-*

poraine: „Les thèmes d'Arthur Schnitzler sont sentimentaux ou frôlent le scabreux; il connaît tous les effets de théâtre et en use sans vergogne; il a la rouerie du boulevardier. Cependant sa réputation d'écrivain superficiel ou immoral est fort injuste."[20]

Das Wien, dem Schnitzler entstammt und ohne das er nicht gedacht werden kann, ist nicht ganz die Stadt der Zuckerbäcker und der allgegenwärtigen Liebesverhältnisse. Wien war in seiner Geschichte stets, und ist es bis auf den heutigen Tag geblieben, die Wasserscheide zwischen entgegengesetzten Welten. Schon das alte Vindobona war im Zuge des Donaulimes der Römer befestigt worden und stellte die Grenze des römischen Reiches gegen den barbarischen Norden dar. Und später trotzte es zweimal dem Ansturm der Türken und vor seinen Toren prallten Ost und West schicksalshaft zusammen. Sogar heute noch, oder schon wieder, stellt Wien die Grenze zwischen Ost und West dar und der Volksspruch: „Gleich hinter Wien fangt der Balkan an" ist gültig wie eh und je. Dieses Wien war im Zuge des 19. und im Beginn des 20. Jahrhunderts die Stätte schwerer sozialer und politischer Spannungen und die Sammelstelle heterogener Bevölkerungselemente. Die Wiener ahnten die kommende Bedrohung und sehnten sich nach dem Glück, an das sie nur schwer glauben konnten. Schnitzler hat diesen Rahmen und das von ihm Eingeschlossene benützt, um das Ewig-Menschliche und Allgemein-Gültige durch das Medium der ihm am besten bekannten Typen darzustellen. Das er nicht wirklich milieugebunden war, hat er durch solche Meisterwerke wie den *grünen Kakadu, Geronimo, Schleier der Beatrice, Paracelsus*, und andere, bewiesen.

Die Franzosen sehen Schnitzler als sich geistig mehr verwandt als den Deutschen. Besonders auch in der Beschwingtheit seiner Form. Aber die Botschaft, die er bringt, verstehen sie ebenso wenig wie die Deutschen. Denn auch sie verwechseln Leichtheit mit Seichtheit. Es ist Aufgabe der Schnitzler-Forschung auch hier aufklärend zu wirken.

[1] *Arthur Schnitzler, eine Studie* (Hamburg, 1911), p. 7
[2] *Op. cit.*, p. 25.
[3] Wien, 1954, p. 12.
[4] Salzburg, 1951, p. 431.
[5] Wien, Knepler, p. 10.
[6] Bern, 1956, p. 25.
[7] G. S. Viereck. *Glimpses of the Great* (New York, 1930), p. 407.
[8] *Op. cit.*, p. 88.
[9] R. F. Arnold. *Das moderne Drama* (Strassburg, 1908), pp. 237, 239 quoted by Bergel, *op. cit.*, p. 185.
[10] May 15, pp. 419-423.
[11] *Journal of English and Germanic Philology* XXII, pp. 376-411.
[12] Nov. 12, 1922, p. 657.
[13] *PMLA*, XLVIII, pp. 209-219.
[14] IV, pp. 339-354.
[15] „Arthur Schnitzler." Année 16, part 3, pp. 813-830.
[16] Paris, 1908, p. 229.
[17] Paris, pp. 112-114.
[18] Paris, 1936.
[19] Neuchâtel, 1948.
[20] F. Mossé, ed. *La Littérature allemande* (Paris), pp. 806-807.

IN FRANZÖSISCHER SPRACHE ERSCHIENENE WERKE ARTHUR SCHNITZLERS

Anatole, suivi de *La compagne*. Traductions de Maurice Rémon et Maurice Vaucaire. Paris, Stock, 1913 (Bibliothèque cosmopolite no. 70).

L'appel des ténèbres, suivi de *La flûte du pâtre* et de *Le Lieutenant Gustl*. Traduction de Suzanne Clauser. Préface de Paul Géraldy. Paris, Stock, 1932.

– Ibid., 1932 (Le cabinet cosmopolite, no. 64).

La compagne, drame en un acte, 1904, Paris, Revue politique et littéraire.

Les dernières cartes, Nouvelle trad. de l'allemand par Dominique Auclères. Paris, Calmann-Lévy, 1935 (Collection: Traduit de ...).

Liebelei (*Amourette*), pièce en trois actes traduite de l'allemand par Suzanne Clauser.– Paris, l'illustration, 1933 (La petite illustration, revue hebdomadaire, no. 548, théâtre, no. 335).

Mademoiselle Else, traduit de l'allemand par Clara Pollaczek, Paris, Stock 1926, 2me e.d. 1929 (Le cabinet cosmopolite no. 9).

Mademoiselle Else (Traduction de Clara K. Pollaczek), suivie de plusieurs nouvelles traduites de l'allemand par Suzanne Clauser: *Le destin du baron de Leisenbohg, Fleurs, Géronimo l'aveugle et son frère. L'assassin, L'apothéose, Les morts se taisent.* Paris, Stock, 1932. (Le roman cosmopolite).

Mourir. Traduit de l'allemand par Gaspar Valette. Lausanne, Payot et Paris, Perrin et Cie., 1896.

La pénombre des âmes, nouvelles traduites de l'allemand par Suzanne Clauser. Préface de Félix Berteaux. Paris, Stock, 1929 (Le cabinet cosmopolite no. 41) Contient: *Le destin du Baron de Leisenbogh, Fleurs, Géronimo l'aveugle et son frère, Le journal de Radegonde, La mort du vieux garçon, L'assassin, L'ombre de Gabriel, L'apothéose, La femme d'un sage, Les morts se taisent.*

Le retour de Casanova, roman traduit de l'allemand par Maurice Rémon. Paris, Neuchâtel, Attinger, 1930.

La ronde, traduction de Maurice Rémon et W. Bauer. Paris, Stock, 1912.

La ronde, dix dialogues, traduits par M. Rémon, W. Bauer et Suzanne Clauser. Paris, Stock, 1931.

Souper d'adieu, comédie en un acte (adaptée par Maurice Vaucaire) Paris, 1905, Ollendorf.

Thérèse, chronique d'une vie de femme, roman traduit de l'allemand par Suzanne Clauser. Préface de Louis Gillet. Paris, A. Michel, 1931. (Collections des maîtres de la littérature étrangère, nouvelle série).

THE MEANING OF DEATH IN SCHNITZLER'S WORK*

by Lore B. Foltin

In the popular image the name of Arthur Schnitzler immediately conjures up visions of old Vienna prior to World War I, the gay metropolis with ist dashing lieutenants of the Imperial Army, its fashionably dressed ladies of high society, and their counterparts, the *süße Mädel*, who live in the suburbs in modest dwellings and who are as refreshing as the rain-washed lilac bushes in their gardens.

For years, critics have spoken of Arthur Schnitzler as a typical representative of the *fin de siècle* art. Epithets such as "tired," "bored," "decadent," "frivolous," "weak," "superficial," "polished," abound in the early criticism of Schnitzler. In the histories of German literature it was – and to a degree it still is – stated that Schnitzler depicts people typical of his hometown, Vienna, *i.e.* people of the Viennese leisure class with too weak a character to cope with the problems of life. Frequently these are men who are flitting from one love affair to another and, incapable of any enduring relationship, end up by dying in a duel or committing suicide.

Subsequently another trend followed in Schnitzler-criticism which might be called, for lack of a better name, psychologism.

* This study was supported in part by a Faculty Fellowship under the Charles E. Merrill Trust.

These critics, of whom the late Otto P. Schinnerer of Columbia University was one of the most perceptive pioneers, were convinced that Schnitzler's strength lies in his unique interest in and portrayal of complex human emotions which he unfolds before his readers as perhaps no other author has done before him.[1]

These critics concerned themselves with such questions as: Was Schnitzler, himself a physician, influenced by Siegmund Freud? Or did the founder of psychoanalysis make his discoveries simultaneously with Schnitzler? Are the dream-sequences, the motifs of hypnosis, and other psychic and para-psychic phenomena which play so prominent a role in Schnitzler's work to be looked upon as literary forerunners of Freud's theories or did Schnitzler turn the Freudian statements into artistic designs?[2] As interesting as the answers to these questions may be, they have little bearing on the actual symbolic content of Schnitzler's work.

In Schnitzler's poetic creations death appears as a central theme.[3] Even a cursory glance at some of his titles reveals this. Among them we find, *Der Tod des Junggesellen, Der tote Gabriel, Der Mörder, Die Toten schweigen, Sterben.*

Today we realize that those critics who lightly treated his works as decadent thrillers or psychic vignettes failed to understand their deeper significance. In Schnitzler's works we find a profound feeling of distrust toward the secure statements the late nineteenth century had made concerning politics, social institutions, art, and human behavior in general. For Schnitzler, the individual fate is never less important than the collective fate, which is the reason why he was held to be "not modern" for some time.[4]

The individual fate then, the "I," is Schnitzler's main concern, the total human being, not just the well-defined, rational "ego," but also the rebellious, not conscious, subconscious, unconscious, irrational "id." When we think that even today there is a strong resistance to psychoanalytical theories from many psychologists, as for instance those of the behav-

iorist school, we can understand why literary criticism pro-
tested against such "Freudian" interpretation.[5]

When Schnitzler died in 1931, the concept "modern" had
undergone further changes. But even though Schnitzler's
writings were often undervalued, his portrayals misjudged,
his ideas misconstrued, and his genius was often unrecognized
he himself remained undaunted. This does not mean that he
was at all times impervious to criticism. Indeed, he occasionally
resented the critics of his day. This becomes evident from a
poem published for the first time in Kurt Bergel's edition of
Schnitzler's correspondence with his Danish friend, Georg
Brandes.[6]

Mein Kritiker.

Der Anatol und die Liebelei –
Nichts als sentimentale Plauderei.
Die Frau des Weisen und andere Novellen
Ich sagt' es seit jeher: Nur Bagatellen!
Beatrice? gar Verse! nun hat er vertan –
Der Weg ins Freie? ein Judenroman.
Der Kakadu? bestenfalls Variété –
Das Zwischenspiel? wieder nur Liebesweh.
Der einsame Weg und das weite Land –?
Psychologie aus zweiter Hand.
Der Reigen – wir wissen ja – Schweinerein,
Marionetten? aha, jetzt gesteht er es ein.
Der Ruf des Lebens? bum, Spekulation.
Medardus–? Ausstattungssensation.
Bernhardi, pfui Teufel, ein Thesenstück
Und ohne Weiber, er geht zurück.
Komödie der Worte – die schreibt er ja immer
Nur freilich wird's mit den Jahren schlimmer. –
Was bin ich für ein Mann ihm gegenüber!
Was er auch schreiben mag, ich schreibe drüber.

In a letter to his young friend and admirer Franz Werfel, Schnitzler said that he wrote of timeless topics, of love and death. These indeed are the core of his work, – with multifaceted variations such as befits an imaginative mind. To substantiate this, literary criticism had to overcome the false notions that his work is mainly a Viennese *Stimmungsbild,* and that its interest lies in its anticipation of or concurrence with the discoveries of psychoanalysis.

Schnitzler, for all his polished elegance of style, looked behind smug surfaces, he opened sluices, he exposed, however obliquely, corruption and horror. He saw and he showed that it is possible for love and hate, boldness and timidity, courage and fear to dwell side by side in the same heart. More than that: that these opposites can be related in a strange sort of way, reflecting what Freud called overcompensation. Max, the rationalist in the cycle *Anatol* knows that when he says to his friend, Anatol, in *Abschiedssouper,* "Ich weiß, du behandelst sie brutal ... Als wenn das nicht auch eine Art von Verwöhnen wäre."[7] Rademacher knows it, when in *Die letzten Masken* he remarks, "... aber was ist denn alle Glut, mit der man ein geliebtes Wesen erwartet gegen die Sehnsucht nach einem, den man haßt ..."[8] And behind all this, behind love, the fleeting, the possessive, the imagined love, and behind hate, the cold hate of revenge or the burning anger, there is death, ever present, even in the midst of life. Death casts a shadow over all the creatures of Schnitzler's imagination; death is present during the passionate embraces as well as the daring and frivolous games that many of his characters play. It can be sudden death, a self-inflicted death, the slow death which comes to the aging, or the death issuing from boredom, a sense of uselessness, hopelessness.

What is the meaning of death in Schnitzler's work? Bernhard Blume flatly denies that death has any meaning for Schnitzler: "Schnitzler stellt in den Mittelpunkt seines Weltbildes den Tod aber er weigert sich, ihm einen Sinn zu geben."[9] Another critic, Herbert Lederer, recently claimed, "Just as the satisfaction of the sexual urge gives a short-lived release from the oppressive feeling of loneliness, so is the ever-constant threat of death its ultimate horror – death the inescapable pinnacle of utmost, unspeakable loneliness."[10] This statement points in the same direction as Franz Werfel's pronouncement, "Schnitzler sieht nicht – wie ihm seit manchem Jahrzehnt die Kritik nachsagt – den Tod als Arzt; er sieht ihn als Ethiker. In dem vielleicht unbewußten System seiner Weltanschauung bedeutet Tod die Strafe der Einsamkeit, für das Nichtgelebthaben."[11]

Robert O. Weiss holds, "The psychologist Schnitzler utilizes death like the forces of love and sex: to motivate his characters into interesting, realistic behavior."[12]

All of these views seem to overlook that other aspect of death, as treated by Schnitzler, namely that rather than always being the inescapable pinnacle of loneliness or the punishment thereof, death is often inseparably linked with the theme of man's purification.

Death appears to us thus from two sides, that of the surviving and that of the dying. Those about to die sometimes rise in the last moments of their lives to a certain greatness; one might even say they rise to the challenge of death. In one of Schnitzler's one-act plays – a literary form in which he excelled – *Die letzten Masken*, the dying journalist Karl Rademacher has plotted revenge on a friend of his youth, the successful writer Weihgast. Rademacher sends for this man on the last evening of his life and begs him to visit him in the hospital. He plans to humble the smug Weihgast by revealing that he had committed adultery with his wife, and to insult him in every possible manner. When Weihgast appears, however, he spends his time with him in small talk; he dismisses the desire for revenge. The approach of death has rendered such revenge small, foolish, insignificant. "Was hat unsereiner mit

39

den Leuten zu schaffen, die morgen auch noch auf der Welt sein werden?"[13] he asks. Death's proximity imports to Rademacher a nobility he lacked previously.

In the drama *Der einsame Weg,* the following dialogue occurs:
Johanna: "Warum reden Sie denn vom Sterben?"
Sala: "Gibst es einen anständigen Menschen, der in irgendeiner guten Stunde in tiefster Seele an etwas anderes denkt?" And the same Stefan von Sala says to Dr. Reumann, "Nein, Sie sollen mir meine Todesstunde nicht wegeskamotieren!"[14] This is an implicit anticipation of the sanative power of death.

Death as the great mitigator of human grief, the healer of human melancholy, and thus, the extreme opposite of the "pinnacle of loneliness" since it brings relief from it, assumes a dominant role in Schnitzler's work.

Perhaps the most famous of his novellas is *Leutnant Gustl,* if for no other reason than because of its "inner monologue" technique which in more recent times in German literature has been successfully employed by such writers as, e.g., Heinrich Böll. After a concert Lieutenant Gustl has been offended by a baker, who, because of his profession, is not *satisfaktionsfähig.* Gustl sees no other way out of the quandary than to take his own life. He spends his last night walking through the streets of Vienna, reflecting on a park bench, even stepping into a church during early mass. Then he stops for a last breakfsat in a coffee house where he learns, to his immense relief, that the baker died of a stroke during the night. This means to Gustl that he can live. Certainly, Gustl is anything but a tragic hero, regardless of the more fortunate turn of events for him. Of interest here, however, is that the little lieutenant with whom we become acquainted in the course of the night through many loosely shaped mental pictures and half formulated thoughts presented in a flash-back technique – that this little lieutenant with his rather primitive notions of love, order, and above all, honor, nevertheless prepares to die in a forthright manner, which, as Herbert Cysarz so aptly put it, "im

40

größeren Ernstfall vielleicht zur Tapferkeit würde."[15] Only death can cleanse Leutnant Gustl from his guilt. Indeed we are reminded of the words of Tennyson in "The Charge of the Light Brigade,"

> Theirs not to reason why
> Theirs but to do and die.[16]

Further indication of Schnitzler's positive attitude toward imminent death may be seen in the novella *Casanovas Heimfahrt*. Schnitzler depicts a duel between the aging Casanova and his youthful, virile rival, lieutenant Lorenzi. While the duel has been motivated by quite ordinary reasons, *i.e.* gambling debts and a woman, the manner in which the men duel is quite extraordinary. The opponents fence in the nude. In this, it would appear, Schnitzler indicates that life's external exigencies and petty concerns have been stripped away. Thus both men meet soul to soul.

After Lorenzi has taken off his clothes, he addresses Casanova with the simple statement, "Ich bin bereit, Herr Chevalier!"[17] And as if to underline this total readiness, Schnitzler adds, "Alles Gemeine war aus seinem Antlitz weggelöscht; er schien so bereit zu töten als zu sterben."[18]

When we view death from the other perspective, that is of the survivors, it assumes a different appearance. It now serves to intensify the awareness of the beauty and sweetness of life.

In the beginning of the poignant novella *Sterben*, Marie, the mistress of a young man who has but one year to live, believes she wants to die with her lover. "Ich will mit dir sterben." "Ich kann ohne dich nicht sein."[19] When the time comes for him to die, however, and he, unable to bear the fact that Marie will live on, wants to take her with him, she cries out, "Nein, nein. Ich will nicht!"[20] and runs away. In spite of her lover's death, life is worth living for Marie.

Further it is possible for death to augment the bond between those remaining, as for example in the drama *Der einsame Weg*. A poignant expression of this idea is uttered by Wegrath, who, addressed as "Vater!" by his foster-son Felix after the suicide of his daughter, becomes upset and exclaims emotionally, "Müssen solche Dinge geschehen, daß mir dieses Wort klingt, als hört ichs zum erstenmal ...?"[21] Death has strengthened the love between Felix and the man who has reared him.

In the novella *Frau Berta Garlan* we read, "Es war ihr einen Augenblick, als hätte ihr eigenes Schicksal nur den einen Sinn gehabt, sie das Elend dieses Mannes ganz verstehen zu machen."[22] Here too death has brought about a bond of understanding.

Death may even establish a bond between the living and the dead, when such a bond did not exist while both were alive. The novella *Casanovas Heimfahrt* illustrates this beautifully in the scene when Casanova, before leaving his dead opponent bends down to the man whom he has just killed and kisses him on the forehead. "Wie zu einem letzten Opfer beugte er sich nochmals nieder und drückte dem Toten die Augen zu."[23]

It would far exceed the range of our specific topic to show the relationship between death and sleep in Schnitzler's work, or a similar relationship in the work of a poet of an entirely different complexion such as Gottfried Benn, but perhaps it is well to remind ourselves of these relationships even if only in passing.

In summing up we may say that while Schnitzler's work must be understood against its peculiar geographical, psychological and sociological background and is thus more culture-bound perhaps than many other works of art, its appeal is universal. Or is it because of it? It may be, that in portraying the Austrian bourgeois landscape of the mind of his era so authentically and perfectly, he caught the threads leading into future literary developments, *i.e.*, threads leading directly to Benn, Anouilh, Frisch, and Ionesco.[24]

In Schnitzler's work, we have tried to point out, death may play the dual role of purifying and setting men free on the one hand, and of unifying and strengthening a bond on the other

42

hand. With his preoccupation with death Schnitzler is linked with a tradition in German literature which goes back as far as Gottfried von Straßburg's *Tristan*, where we first encounter the dichotomy between "Lebensinstinkt," and "Todesinstinkt," if these Freudian terms may be used. This dichotomy is echoed through Schnitzler's work, who knew, like his contemporary Yeats:

> For wisdom is the property of the dead,
> A something incompatible with life ...[25]

NOTES

[1] See Otto P. Schinnerer, "The Early Works of Arthur Schnitzler," *Germanic Review*, IV (1929), 153-197.

[2] See W. Dehorn, "Psychoanalyse und neuere Dichtung," *Germanic Review*, VII (1932), 245-262.
Victor A. Oswald, Jr. and Veronica Pinter Mindess, "Schnitzler's 'Fräulein Else' and the Psychoanalytic Theory of Neuroses," *Germanic Review*, XXVI (1951), 279-288.
Frederick J. Beharriell, "Schnitzler's Anticipation of Freud's Dream Theory," *Monatshefte*, XLV (1953), 81-89.
See further the penetrating analysis of Heinz Politzer, "Diagnose und Dichtung," *Forum*, IX. Jahr (1962), 217-219, 266-270.

[3] After the completion of her article, the author became acquainted with Robert O. Weiss' Master's thesis, *Death in the Works of Arthur Schnitzler*, University of Missouri, 1951. Weiss compiled some interesting statistics. In 61 of 97 works considered, he found a total of 120 individual deaths (p. 33), the most frequent cause being suicide, followed, in that order, by murder, duel, execution, accident, and war (p. 35).

[4] *Cf.* Alfred Biese, *Deutsche Literaturgeschichte, Dritter Band*, C. H. Beck'sche Verlagsbuchhandlung, München, 1930, p. 565. „Heute wirkt das Stück *Reigen* , wie überhaupt die Atmosphäre des Schnitzlerschen Werkes, schon etwas überlebt und altmodisch."

[5] *Cf.* Leon Edel, "Criticism and Psychoanalysis: Notes on the two disciplines," *Chicago Review*, 15 (1961), 100-109. Edel does not deal with Schnitzler, but his observations are pertinent for the Schnitzler reader.

[6] *Georg Brandes und Arthur Schnitzler*, University of California Press,

Publications in Modern Philology, XLVI, Berkeley and Los Angeles, 1956, p. 40.

[7] Schnitzler, *Gesammelte Werke*, I, S. Fischer Verlag, Berlin, 1918, p. 61 .(Hereafter cited as *Werke*.)

[8] *Ibid.*, II, p. 381.

[9] *Das Weltbild Arthur Schnitzlers*, Knöller, Stuttgart, 1936, p. 17.

[10] "Arthur Schnitzler: A Chronicle of Loneliness," *The German Quarterly*, XXX (1957), 82-94.

[11] "Arthur Schnitzler zu seinem 60. Geburtstag," *Die neue Rundschau*, XXIII (1922), 509-510.

[12] *Op. cit.*, p. 72.

[13] *Werke*, II, p. 390.

[14] *Werke*, III, p. 17 and p. 61.

[15] "Das Imaginäre in der Dichtung Arthur Schnitzlers," *Wissenschaft und Weltbild*, 13. Jhg. (1960), 102-112.

[16] *Poetical Works*, Thomas E. Crowell, New York and Boston, 1851, p. 170.

[17] *Gesammelte Schriften*, IV, p. 356.

[18] *Ibid.*, p. 356.

[19] *Werke*, I, p. 18.

[20] *Ibid.*, p. 114.

[21] *Werke*, III, p. 103.

[22] *Werke*, II. p, 181.

[23] *Gesammelte Schriften*, IV, p. 357.

[24] *Cf.* Dr. Wolfgang Kraus, "Wir spielen immer, wer es weiß, ist klug," *Neue Württembergische Zeitung*, 5. Mai 1962.

[25] "Blood and the Moon," *The Collected Poems*, MacMillan, London, 1934, p. 269.

THE IMAGE OF THE AUSTRIAN
IN ARTHUR SCHNITZLER'S WRITINGS

by Robert A. Kann

An attempt to discuss the impact of Schnitzler's home country
on his literary work requires some clarifications from the
outset. They pertain just as much to topical limitations of this
essay as to its extension beyond purely literary aspects. In a
fair number of writings on Austrian history I have never yet
attempted to define the concept of Austrian man in psychological terms, since such an unprovable definition would be
controversial by necessity. Furthermore the Austrian problem
in Schnitzler's work refers to the German cultural orbit but –
and this modification is important – to its position within the
plethora of the multinational Habsburg empire. How far one
or the other, the German or the multinational factor, deter-
mines the Autrian character cannot be discussed in abstracto,
particularly since we have to deal here not with Austrian man
as he was in Schnitzler's lifetime, but as Schnitzler saw him.

As to another restriction, I propose here to survey only a
mere selection of Schnitzler's dramatic and prose work, and
this not even primarily for obvious reasons of space. In a sense
all of a writer's work represents distinctive features of his home
land where he was born and died, and the greater a writer is,
the better would he be able to convey its atmosphere to his
readers through his works. Moreover, if such a writer, like

Schnitzler, belongs to the very elite of the literary impressionism of the last pre-World-War I generation, the result should be manifest. The extreme sensibility of the great poets of that era for the impact of impressions from the outside world changes their whole life-work into a repository of countless associations linked to home, country and land of the fathers. To be sure, the concept of impressionism does by no means cover to the full the essence of all, or perhaps any, of Schnitzler's writings. Yet, as far as impressionist influences and techniques are manifest, all of Schnitzler's work and all to the same degree could be subject to our analysis. Quite clearly this would deprive this essay of much of its specific significance and thus some yardstick of selections will have to be applied. Before we turn from the restrictive factors in our reflections, the lack of a definition of Austrian man and that of comprehensiveness in regard to the survey of Schnitzler's work, we also have to face the needs for extension beyond the purely literary sphere. We have to turn to the political and social problems of his time and place. We have to probe at least in the most general terms how far they exercised a particularly important influence on his life work.

Schnitzler has always and rightly been considered an outstanding type of the non-political writer, and there is no doubt about it that his major works from *Der Weg ins Freie* in 1908 over *Professor Bernhardi* to *Über Krieg und Frieden*, written during the first World War, and finally *Buch der Sprüche und Bedenken* of 1927, abound in the expression of extreme aversion to politics. Party politics at that! Inasmuch as Schnitzler believed in the ideals of humanitarianism and the unimpeded freedom of the individual in a humane society conscious of the dignity of every single individual, he may well be called a political man in the noble and pure Aristotelian sense. This means the concern with and the faith in man and his social obligations in a spiritually free society. It is this very issue which he sees increasingly endangered in the Austria of his youth and the prime of his manhood. It is still this problem he is finally concerned with in the Austria of his old age. In his work it is still the dual-monarchy of old. With few exceptions, his major post-World-War writings such as *Therese, Spiel im Morgengrauen* and *Flucht in die Finsternis,* to name only a few outstanding ones, still have their setting in the Habsburg empire where Schnitzler had all his roots.

To return to politics in the very mundane sense in which Schnitzler saw them, what are the specific issues within the bygone multinational Great Power of deep concern to an unpolitical man like Arthur Schnitzler? First there is the national struggle between the Austro-Germans and the other nationalities which dominated the political scene in the last half-century of the monarchy's existence. True, Schnitzler refers to this struggle only seldom. Yet inasmuch as the nationality conflict led in turn to the radicalisation and increasing intolerance of Austrian political life altogether, it represents in a way a foundation of Schnitzler's dissatisfaction with changes in the environmental setting. To be somewhat more specific, Schnitzler is deeply concerned with the decline of Liberalism of the time of his father; although this Liberalism was anchored in German culture, he wished to see it supranational rather than outright national in its political philosophy. He is disturbed by the rise of a radical Pan Germanism which from its small beginning in the eighteen-eighties dominates increasingly broad sectors of intellectual and particularly of academic life. He is hardly less worried about the rise of a political clericalism in the frame of the Christian Social party which, as he understands its program and actions, fights intellectual life altogether. Furthermore its political strength is anchored in the rising social force of the urban petty bourgeoisie. Schnitzler perceives this social class – *Der Weg ins Freie* and, projected into the future, *Der junge Medardus* to wit – as hostile to his system of intellectual values. To be very sure, such value judgments pertain to more or less organized groups only, never in any af Schnitzler's writings to individuals just because they belong to a certain social or even political group. Nobody even faintly conversant with the young Dr. Pflugfelder or the priest in *Professor Bernhardi* could seriously entertain such a proposition. Yet this impartiality applies not only to conceivable political opponents. A look at the hollow and glib editor-in-chief in the comedy *Fink und Fliederbusch,* to name only one example of several, makes it just as clear that Schnitzler never extolls a phony kind of pseudo-liberalism because it may meet his own personal interests to a point.

Closely interrelated with the issue of Pan-Germanism and Clericalism is for Schnitzler the ugly problem of anti-Semitism which stands in the foreground of his major prose work, *Der Weg ins Freie,* and indirectly in one of his outstanding plays, the so-called political comedy *Professor Bernhardi.* Deeply as Schnitzler personally felt about this question, two points may be easily overlooked. For once the problem is very clearly treated as primarily one of general human and not of specific Jewish concern. This is indicated by the controversial but certainly supra-denominational religious issue in the play, as well as by the vantage point from which the problem of anti-Semitism is viewed in the novel – namely its primary reflection in the eyes of a Gentile and not of a Jew. Secondly it is notable that this question was discussed by Schnitzler at length only in two works written in 1908 and 1912. In substance he had not dealt with it before, he did not return to it afterwards, though external reasons to be concerned with the question unfortunately were never fully lacking during his lifetime. It stands to reason that Schnitzler felt he had said what he wanted to say on the issue and felt there was nothing to add to it nor to take away. If anti-Semitism may thus perhaps be called a central issue in Schnitzler's relationship to the outside world in his work it appears only as one facet of a general human problem.

48

From a discussion of Schnitzler's environment we must not exclude problems which he seemingly ignored, since such omissions also help us in a way to focus his life work. The major political issue of the day which is notably absent from the social spectrum of Schnitzler's world is the rise of organized labor by way of the Austrian Social Democratic party. It coincides almost with that of the Christian-Social-petty-bourgeois movement and follows rather closely the spread of radical German nationalism. The fact that the rise of labor is not reflected in Schnitzler's writings certainly is not due to any aversion to the then underprivileged classes in society, nor can it be attributed to the outworn cliché concept of his alleged concentration on death, dream, and love. Even the assumption that rejection of organized mass movements of any kind by the supreme individualist Schnitzler is the decisive factor would be an oversimplification. Far more suggestive is another interpretation. Schnitzler is concerned with the issue of politics in the modern sense only as far as he is compelled to take a stand against it, in particular radical nationalism, intolerance, irrationalism, hostility to cultural progress and anti-Semitism. Wherever political conflict does not disturb his world and his system of values, he stands aside. That seems to be the case with the labor movement. Schnitzler's lack of concern with the problems of the Fourth Estate is thus surely not to be interpreted as antipathy toward industrial labor as such, though it is, of course, part of his general dislike for politics.[1]

Yet a political man, even in his purest form, is of course not free from the impact of the *Zeitgeist* as reflected in his environment. The world of Schnitzler, as he saw it, is no exception. And here it is important to note that the literary re-creation of this world is largely concerned with the type of man whom Schnitzler knew from first-hand observation, close to his parental bourgeois world. This eliminates labor in the same natural way as it excludes the whole hierarchy of rural

Austria from any but the viewpoint of the summer guest and tourist.

Yet, as noted at a later point, lack or abundance of personal experience and observation is here only one factor. Emphasis on the urban bourgeois order and exclusion of others does not aim at the photogenic reproduction of environmental factors. Rather we face here a reality which proceeds from re-creation of the external world to the higher reality of the spirit. In this sense the center of gravity in Schnitzler's Austrian world rests, so to speak, a little to the right of center in the urban upper bourgeoisie, with a strong sprinkling of the professional classes, primarily the writer, the scholar, the M.D., frequently in the combination of the doctor in his double capacity as physician and academic teacher. Of course the portraying of the doctor as the wise, usually fatherly and with few exceptions[2] loyal friend, quite clearly relates to Schnitzler's associations with his own father and in a wider sense with psychoanalysis which plays so important a part in his lifework. Yet, I see also a typically Austrian connection in the conspicuous role the physician assumes in so many of Schnitzler's works. The doctor represents wisdom, kindness and truth, and wherever he is present one cannot speak of a purely negative evaluation of Austrian public life as seen by some of Schnitzler's interpreters.

In a sense the counterweight to the doctor in Schnitzler's world is the officer, who is frequently but not as frequently portrayed as the physician, and usually perceived as weak, shallow and chained to prejudices. This does not indicate an unsympathetic treatment by any means, but inasmuch as the officer played a dominant social role in the feudal tradition of the Habsburg empire, his forced obedience to an anachronistic code of honor serves as a kind of symbol for the decline of the dual monarchy which is perceived as tied to outworn values.

I would not presume to suggest similar qualified generalizations in regard to the upper bourgeoisie, the stratum from

50

which more of Schnitzler's principal characters are recruited than from any other group. But it is perhaps fair to suggest that, taken as a group, they are not viewed in a more kindly light than the petty bourgeoisie, although single individuals in either group are just as often respected and admired. Perhaps the main difference rests in the fact that in the time of Schnitzler's manhood the upper bourgeoisie is not perceived as a clearly accentuated group, whereas the urban petty bourgeoisie could be focussed in a much more specific sense. The latter, as will be remembered, was then very largely tied to a movement in conflict with Schnitzler's concepts of reason and tolerance.

Sharply, in fact even more sharply profiled is the aristocracy which differs from any other social group, though its problems resemble to a point those of the officer. The officer is seen as representative of an anachronistic system in which he often tragically collides with a world he never made. The aristocrat is likewise considered as out of step with the spirit of his time and place. At the same time he is looked at with faint amusement and irony, frequently with a trace of sympathy and even respect for quite a few aspects of his waning world.

Finally the artist, above all the actor, the musician and the writer appear frequently in Schnitzler's prose as well as in his dramatic work, and usually lend it additional color. While this is often "local color," the image of the artist and his creative qualities transcend by far the local and even the national stage. In a sense the writer, more precisely perhaps the literate, represents here the exception to the rule. Sometimes, like in *Der einsame Weg*, he is pictured as a truly tragic personality in conflict with himself. At other times, like in *Der Weg ins Freie*, he is seen as tragicomically torn between self-observation, self-pity, and hypersensitivity. More frequently, like in *Reigen, Literatur, Das weite Land*, and *Fink und Fliederbusch*, his hollow vanity is persiflaged. I do not think this can be explained away by the self-debunking process so typical of intellectuals and here particularly of literary men. The somewhat outworn issue of the inferiority complex is probably not at stake either. Rather we seem to find at the very roots of this attitude a kind of general unhappiness with the Austrian intellectual climate, with, as Schnitzler sees it, a lack of respect for the writer as the undaunted champion of truth; this unhappiness extends also to the many opportunities offered the small literary man to corrupt taste and truth. Here is one of the few points where Schnitzler comes close to the views of Karl Kraus for whom he otherwise had little use.[3]

As noted in the introductory statement to this essay, all of Schnitzler's work reveals the influence of his home country and in particular the city of his birth and death, Vienna. This is just as true for the Renaissance tragedy, *Der Schleier der Beatrice*, with its setting in Bologna as, for instance, for the play, *Der Ruf ins Leben*, which is loosely tied to the Austrian Piedmontese conflicts in 1848/49. One shows as much as the other Schnitzler's deep feeling about the right to live one's own life, the position of the artist in society, and the ever-present threat of death. It would be a shallow and philistine approach indeed to claim that Austrian man appears more clearly in Schnitzler's work just because specific reference is made to an Austrian setting. There is little doubt that in all of his writing man comes first and the local color interwoven in his characterization, second. In some of his works, however, this local or national character is more closely connected with the problems of the work and its characters than in others. Whether Austria or Vienna is referred to specifically may be accidental. On this basis we have to make our selection and, strict as it is, we have to make it even stricter by concentrating, with few exceptions, on main works.

The social character and in a sense the social problems of Schnitzler's Austrian world seem to me particularly clearly, but by no means exclusively, represented in the following works listed here in two groups chronologically. We think here first of the plays *Liebelei* (1896), *Freiwild* (1896), *Reigen* (1900), the one-act sketch *Literatur* (1901)[4], *Komtesse Mitzi* (1907) and *Das weite Land* (1911). With the exception of *Freiwild* and *Komtesse Mitzi* which in our context have a significance of their own, all these plays rank among Schnitzler's outstanding works. The same is true for the novels and stories *Frau Berta Garlan* (1900), *Leutnant Gustl* (1901), *Therese* (1928), *Fräulein Else* (1929) and *Spiel im Morgengrauen* (1931).[5] Quite clearly, and perhaps partly due to a transitory change in public taste and a by-no-means merely transitory gradual withdrawal from the world, Schnitzler, after 1918, had turned increasingly from the lively world of the stage to the quiet atmosphere in which he created his late novels and stories.

Finally we will have to reflect on a third small group of works which come closer to the portrayals and problems of Austrian man than any other, the novel *Der Weg ins Freie* of 1909 and the plays *Der junge Medardus* (1909) and *Professor Bernhardi* (1912).

To be sure, there are a number of outstanding works by Schnitzler not included in these groups, and just as surely the issues traced in the following discussion are not the only ones and by no means necessarily the most important ones in these works. What is in question here is not depth or beauty *per se* but the relationship to an Austrian image.

To begin with, the plays *Liebelei* and *Freiwild* and the stories and/or novels *Leutnant Gustl* and *Spiel im Morgengrauen* bring out a variety of themes and characters. They have in common that the plot of all of them is focussed on problems arising from the military code of honor and its use or rather abuse to protect false values. In one case, *Liebelei*, Schnitzler's most beautiful tragedy of love, a duel fought for the sake of a purely conventional matter of honor destroys the lives of the pair of lovers from different classes of society. The scion of the upper bourgeoisie is bound to submit to this strait jacket, the young woman from the lower middle-class in her simple human feelings cannot grasp the necessity. Class differences of a somewhat similar nature play their part also in the love affair of *Freiwild*, where the fatal duel is avoided but not its consequences. The reason here is again a bowing to convention, in this case fear of seeming afraid. Fear of being suspected of fear is also in essence the dramatic key issue in *Leutnant Gustl*; here the semi-tragic situation, which eventually leads to an end that is as happy as it is dubious, emphasizes only the hollowness of the problem which faces the officer. And again, in *Spiel im Morgengrauen*, the young lieutenant who pays with his life for his inability to pay his gambling debts and therewith saves his honor, is a victim of a deadly convention. In all these works, though not to the same degree of artistic accomplishment, the problem of ambivalence of honor does not encompass the full richness of feeling and creative power shown by the poet, but in all of them the issue implies something far more weighty than the conflict situation between the military and the civilian world. At stake here is the whole social system of the Habsburg empire. Neither in rational nor in human terms does this system meet the responsibilities of the time. The society which believes in it is doomed to fail and to fall, and the sunset beauty of a waning age, deeply felt by Schnitzler, heightens the tragedy.

It would have been suggestive to add *Das weite Land* to this group, since here too a duel linked to the issue of military convention plays a fatal part. Yet the duel here is neither the central theme nor is it pictured as an absurdity in the same sense as in the other works. It is used as a cruel device to repair a social prestige damaged and at the same time stimulated by erotic license. One of the major themes of this often misunderstood work of unsurpassed depth of thought and subtlety of characterization is to show the almost vicious shallowness of the upper bourgeoisie of the last years of peace before the outbreak of the great war. The very idea of *Das weite Land,* the unpredictability of the human soul and the demands of the subconscious, transcends, of course, any national or social theme though this play, with its setting in a small spa near Vienna and an elegant hotel in the South Tyrolian Dolomites, is particularly strong in local Austrian colors. But not primarily for this reason is it associated here with an image of Austrian man. The sterility of an upper-middle-class society turned loose, in this play, in the field of sexual relations is shown by the absence of any ideological issue worth fighting for. The ethical nihilism of these people represents perhaps in a way Schnitzler's anxiety about the deserved decline of an Austrian social group to which he himself was tied with so many fibers of his nature.

Fräulein Else, technically the counterpart of *Leutnant Gustl* almost a generation before it, deals with the same world in the same setting of flirtation, lust, the recklessness of the gambler and cowardice in facing social consequences. Obviously Schnitzler had not changed his opinion about the society of the last pre-war decades, but there may be a symbolic significance in the fact that the innocent victims – a young naval officer in *Das weite Land,* a young society girl in *Fräulein Else* – represent a class which cannot plead innocence but perhaps ignorance of its own faults.

Another group of works, or perhaps more correctly two merged into one, includes the two one-act sketches, *Komtesse Mitzi* and *Literatur,* the full length play *Zwischenspiel,*[6] and the short novel *Frau Berta Garlan.* Admittedly these four works make strange bedfellows and can be lumped together only for our specific purpose. *Komtesse Mitzi,* most definitely written in a clear comedy style, and *Zwischenspiel,* the noble play about the marriage problems of the artist, one of the most subtle of Schnitzler's works, both reflect on Austrian aristocracy. True enough, this social order is central to the theme of the sketch and only on the fringe of the drama. Yet in both of them, though in the sketch in a much more pronounced manner, Schnitzler looks at aristocracy, decidedly Austrian aristocracy at that, with a kind of sympathetic irony. It is to him a lovable, slightly anachronistic class, not quite adjusted to the demands of the present, but always above petty prejudices. Hofmannsthal's *Der Schwierige* and the princess Werdenberg in *Rosenkavalier* are indeed close relatives of Schnitzler's aristocracy which he considers apparently on the whole as an amiable factor in the declining world of the old empire.

The aristocrat versus the literate, the cavalier of attractive presence and exquisite manners versus the literate, the scribe – today Schnitzler might have said the Beatnik – who is in all and everything the opposite, they are the two male leads in *Literatur*. Here, however, is also a conflict between rather limited brain-power discreetly used, and the forces of a strong intellect tactlessly abused. In hardly any other work of Schnitzler – the none too fortunate satire on journalism, *Fink und Fliederbusch*, possibly excluded, is the travesty of the writer without dignity and psychological chastity so starkly exposed as in this most effective sketch. Yet in the last analysis it is perhaps not quite as funny as it appears on the stage. I have referred previously to Schnitzler's frequently expressed condemnation of the writer as evidence of his dissatisfaction with Austria's intellectual climate, but it may also be indicative of his protest against the excesses of naturalism in the Austrian literary world and of journalism and journalistic techniques in the professional one. Here Schnitzler perceives in his very home-country the unforgivable sin against the spirit more strongly than in any other field.

The point should be made also because artists do appear in all four previously mentioned works, musicians as the main characters in *Zwischenspiel*, a musician also in *Frau Berta Garlan* and a painter in *Komtesse Mitzi*. All of them are pictured in a colorful Austrian setting, though not all of them – the virtuoso in *Frau Berta Garlan* to wit – are perceived as attractive characters. But none of them reveals the obnoxious lack of dignity and reserve which Schnitzler abhors perhaps more than any other human quality. It is an inner quality of shamelessness which is not to be confounded with the naive exhibitionism and vanity of the actor. In the numerous works where Schnitzler is concerned with the actor, above all in the one-act plays *Der grüne Kakadu* (1898), *Stunde des Erkennens* (1915) and *Die letzten Masken* (1901),[7] or the short stories *Der Ehrentag* and *Das neue Lied*, the stage and its cast are sometimes seen with humor, often satirized, but generally respected and viewed with loving concern. Never is the actor pictured as obtrusive and in his very innermost as indecent, as is so frequently the case with the writer. Yet the point at issue here is not so much the unpleasant character of many a writer and the associations of their unpleasantness with the home country. More important seems to me another aspect of the problem. The aversion of the characters in Schnitzler's plays and prose to this indelicacy of the writer reveals that to Schnitzler reserve and a certain shyness are an intrinsic feature of the Austrian character, which is so often obscured by overt friendliness and amiability.

This is perhaps nowhere more apparent than in the last work listed in this group, *Frau Berta Garlan*, which shows the quiet life of a young widow in a small Austrian provincial town, her short and disappointing fling in the world and her quiet withdrawal. Quiet is also the whole setting of this novel, a very unusual one for Schnitzler who not infrequently portrays places outside of the great city as summer resorts. Like its modest patrician class, the town in this novel is different and decidedly dreary. Seen not with arrogance but with that lack of sympathy for the metropolitan petty bourgeoisie and its socially somewhat more elevated projection in the provincial world, the implication is suggestive: true happiness and serenity can never derive from the environment, never from the group, always and only from the human relations to the individual.

Just the same, in this novel the social spectrum of Schnitzler's world widens, and this leads to the two works where it appears even wider, the series of dialogues *Reigen* and the novel *Therese* separated otherwise from each other by a generation in time and much farther in character. In the brilliant scenes of *Reigen*, linked together by the reaction of pairs of lovers to the sexual act, pairs which rise from the bottom of society to its peaks and down to its depths again, one might expect a view of the full circle of the social order. Actually the circle presented by Schnitzler is wide, but by no means all-embracing, and its limitations – the word to be understood here in a merely technical sense – are highly characteristic for Schnitzler

We are again confronted by life in the big city, very decidedly Vienna at that. If we look at the cast of characters as a social ladder rather than as a circle, we find at its bottom the prostitute, at its top the count and cavalry officer. Right in the center is the married couple of upper bourgeois character flanked on the one side by the young gentleman of the same social class and on the other by the grisette who presumably comes from a petty bourgeois environment, just like her sisters in the earlier scenes of *Anatol*. On either wing we find another pair of characters, one from the Bohème artistic element, the poet and the actress, the other a parlor maid and an undefined soldier, obviously from the lower strata of society. All these characters and their actions and responses are drawn with equal mastery, but their position in the social order is by no means equally clearly defined. The prostitute, the soldier, the grisette, but in a sense also the actress, are socially not as clearly focussed as the three central bourgeois figures. They are in a sense appendages linked here by sexual relations directly or indirectly to Schnitzler's Austrian bourgeois world. The whole clearly definable rural sphere with its own social hierarchy lies outside, and the same is true for the large urban industrial labor class.

The situation in the novel *Therese*, the major work of

Schnitzler's old age, is somewhat similar. This melancholic life story of an aging governess is written in minor key and lacks the sparkling wit of *Reigen*, but fully makes up for this lack by the deep sense of social compassion which penetrates the work. Like in *Reigen*, the whole social order is reviewed as far as it has been contacted by this poor woman in the adventures of her gloomy life and shabby love affairs. The life of the officer's daughter is linked to the moderate heights of the upper bourgeoisie, in substance the class of Therese's employers; it descends down to the petty bourgeoisie, of her world between jobs. It touches upon the Bohème, and through Therese's unfortunate son it sinks to the lowest levels of criminal underworld and prostitution. In no other work of Schnitzler is the cruelty and injustice of the social order of the pre-World-War Austrian world as mercilessly shown as in this late masterpiece. The fact that the novel, like all of Schnitzler's works, shies aways from any loud or even any direct program of social demands makes this gripping picture of a wasted life even more moving. Nevertheless, as I see it, there is a kind of social message after Schnitzler's own fashion in this book. The woman who has lost her social status – and here the illegitimate birth of her son serves as a symbol for the uncertainty of her whole life – can never regain it. The bourgeois world of her fiancé, the middle-class environment of her friend the doctor, the Bohème world of her lover, even the underworld of her son, are closed to her. The lesson from *Frau Berta Garlan* is repeated, but accentuated in a social sense. Solutions can never be determined, nay, even be influenced by the cruel social order of the external world, which is of little comfort anyway for the tortures of the human soul. This may be an additional reason why again the clearly visible world of labor and of the rural order is skirted in favor of the gray world between classes. The uncertainties of psychological problems of a frustrated life are merely reflected in the vague fuzziness of the outside world.

Admittedly, another even simpler interpretation would be possible. One might assume, that the gap in Schnitzler's social spectrum of Austria is primarily due to a lack of knowledge beyond his own class on the one hand and a kind of romantic interest in the semi-darkness of artistic and demi-monde interclass relations, as opposed to the rigidity of the clearly defined status of peasantry and labor, on the other. Naturally, like any writer, Schnitzler is at his best, when he can draw on his own experiences and observation and is able to link them to his poetic imagination. Yet this is only one point in the picture. Were this view accepted in full, it would not detract from the greatness of an artist who in that case should be honored as much for the recognition of his limitations as for his wide perception.

And now we must turn to the last and from the standpoint of this analysis the most important group, to the three works created between 1908 and 1912, in the last decade of the empire's existence, the plays *Der junge Medardus* and *Professor Bernhardi* and Schnitzler's major novel, *Der Weg ins Freie*. What distinguishes these works for our purpose is clearly the fact that they convey not only an Austrian atmosphere and Austrian characters, but very specific issues of Austrian public life as well. Whether this factor contributes also to their dominant position in Schnitzler's lifework as a whole, may be open to question, though I for one would tend to believe so. At least two of them have just one more heartstring that ties them to the feeling of Schnitzler's readers than most of his other writings. Reference has already been made to the fact that *Der Weg ins Freie* deals extensively with the position of the Jew in Austria and the problem of anti-Semitism which, from the eighteen-eighties to the nineteen-forties rose there to such hideous forms and proportions. But the Jewish problem, extensively as it is dealt with in all its facets of Jewish assimilation, Jewish conversion on the one hand and Jewish nationalism on the other, is in itself not the main issue and perhaps in a sense not even a direct issue of the novel at all. Anti-Semitism and the Jewish question is rather the screen through which all human feelings, all shades of opinion, are filtered and tested. It would be very difficult to say, and it would go beyond our purpose to establish what comes out best in this test. Certainly it is not extremism, neither nationalism or conversion on the Jewish side, nor Pan-Germanism or political clericalism on that of the gentile. Yet far more important is the disavowal of party politics altogether as an unclean, destructive and bewildering force in public life. It is one aspect of Austrian psychology in Schnitzler which he shares with many of the best Austrians of his times, that party politics is something objectionable in itself which may perhaps be partly excused and modified by a noble purpose, but never be right in essence. The man who follows the star of his life has to renounce these politics in substance as unworthy. He has to do so because their character is determined far more by always objectionable methods than by varying objectives. Can a man of good will, in particular the true artist, fulfill his mission on Austrian soil at all? Schnitzler's attitude on this point is decidedly ambivalent as was that of Grillparzer before him. Austria offers much to the artist in her landscape, her music, indeed in her entire atmosphere, which is featured here perhaps more clearly than in any other of Schnitzler's works. Just the same, the decisive step must be taken into the harsher air beyond her frontiers. Austria favors the rise of talent, but not that of spirit. The rather feeble hero of the novel leaves his country for the sake of his career and sacrifices to this insight the woman of much richer feeling whom he loves. And yet, *Der Weg ins Freie* is permeated by a deep love for Austria, a love that would be unable to make the bitter choice of Georg Wergenthin. This feeling is perhaps best expressed in a marginal character, the aulic Councillor Wilt and his views: "Für ihn aber bedeutete Österreich ein unendlich kompliziertes Instrument, das nur ein Meister richtig behandeln könnte und das nur deshalb so oft übel klänge, weil jeder Stümper seine Kunst daran versuche. ‚Sie werden solange darauf herumschlagen', sagte er traurig, ‚bis alle Saiten zerspringen und der Kasten dazu'."[8]

Professor Bernhardi, chronologically the last in the sequence of these three works on Austrian issues, is much more tightly constructed than the novel, as befits a drama. Again like *Zwischenspiel* it is dubbed a comedy for not quite obvious reasons, though here at least the outcome is not tragic. If in *Der Weg ins Freie* we find a test issue, namely that of anti-Semitism, we are confronted here by a test case. As generally known it is the question whether an attending physician should have the right to bar a priest from administering the sacrament of extreme unction to a patient completely unaware of his imminent death. As Schnitzler sees it, this problem is perceived by the physician, Professor Bernhardi, as a purely human one, but by almost everyone else in the play, at least partly as a political question. This is indeed the position which, very much against the author's intention, has been accepted ever since by a good part of the theater-goers and by the readers of this controversial play. Perhaps just the fact that the characters and their response to the political issues of the last pre-world war years have been portrayed so uncannily true to nature, has contributed to this result. It is most difficult to judge the issues in *Professor Bernhardi* dissociated from their Austrian setting. German nationalism and the ruling political clericalism are shown in a contemptible light, prejudices of a religious, racial and general intellectual nature are rampant. Stronger in emphasis, although not in general philosophy, than *Der Weg ins Freie* is the scathing attack against a wordy and essentially cowardly pseudo-liberalism which claims to take Bernhardi's side but lets him down. Again we find the basic notion that policy, no matter where it stems from and where it heads for, is essentially dirty. We are confronted by another political conclusion as well. The

62

outright opponent of Bernhardi's views, in this case a courageous priest, stands much higher than the false or cowardly friend, whether it is the sorry figure of the vain and phony minister of education or the timid liberal lawyer. The reflection at the end of the fourth act of the play expresses this dogma in Schnitzler's political catechism most succinctly, "... seine Feinde muss man nehmen, wie und wo man sie findet, meine Freunde kann ich mir aussuchen – glücklicherweise..." Such a true friend is the bureaucrat in the play, the ministerial councillor Winkler who sums up "the morale" of the play. Bernhardi asserts that Winkler would have done what Bernhardi did, namely follow his conscience in a specific case without regard to political issues or consequences. This is the answer of the councillor:
"Possibly – in that case, excuse me Professor, I would have been a fool like you."[9]

This is indeed a disturbing conclusion because it transcends by far the issue of religious dogma versus freedom of the individual, where one may well side with the priest. What it means in essence is this: Political life, and in particular Austrian political life, is infested with hollow rhetoric, opportunism, cowardice, prejudice and in a wider sense corruption. The poisonous influence of this political miasma has deeply penetrated into the academic world and into the profession otherwise most respected by Schnitzler, the medical. However the fight against such an Austrian political setup is ridiculed and negated, not so much because it would be an uphill fight but because it simply would not be worth-while. The view that scientific research *per se* is much more important than the fight for laudable social reform on the political level, has already been expressed in *Der Weg ins Freie*[10]. Here similar sentiments are accentuated even more strongly. To enter public life is considered unworthy of the man of high ethical and intellectual standards. This is so, not just because politics are perceived as dirty but also because concern with any questions where one might have to lower one's intellectual standards for the sake of popular support, is considered hypocritical and senseless. As one of the none-too-many upright characters in the play – characters to be found on both sides of the fence – puts it, "Ich finde die Menschen sind im allgemeinen eine recht mangelhafte Gesellschaft, und ich halte mich an die wenigen Ausnahmen da und dort."[11] But public life requires the struggle for the rights of the morally deficient community rather than for those of the few noble exceptions, even though the few may represent on a higher plane the interest of the common good. These exceptional men, as Schnitzler shows again convincingly, are to be found in every camp. Less convincing seems to me the implied questioning of their brave actions in matters of concern to the community, on principle rather than on specific grounds. No service is done to Schnitzler by overlooking the fact that exactly the opposite conclusions can be drawn from this brilliant and depressing play. The notion that the low standards of Austrian politics, as Schnitzler saw them, would give additional justification to the entry of dedicated men into public life, irrespective of the issue at stake, is bypassed, if not refuted.

I do not believe, however, that the conflict of individual versus community as pictured in *Professor Bernhardi* represents the essence of Schnitzler's thinking on Austria and her social world. I strongly feel that the historical drama *Der junge Medardus*, published first in 1909 as Schnitzler's strange contribution to the centenary celebration of Austria's single-handed war against Napoleon, is far more representative in this respect. Preceding *Professor Bernhardi* by three years, the drama covers a much wider range of Austrian life. In this sense it may be permissible to perceive to a point Schnitzler's position in *Professor Bernhardi* as a bitter response to the unhealthy climate in his own professional world of medicine and particularly academic medicine. *Der junge Medardus*, on the other hand, encompasses the Austrian problem as a whole, again in the familiar Viennese setting.

Unquestionably *Der junge Medardus*, the only truly historical play of Schnitzler[12] is still the most misunderstood part of Schnitzler's dramatic work, as the recent performances in the setting of the Schnitzler centennial celebration have shown again. Several factors contribute to this; the tremendous cast, two or, in a way, three none-too-closely interrelated plots, and on the whole a structure far less concentrated and concise than one might expect from the standard master-dramaturgy of Schnitzler. Just the same, I would like to express the very unorthodox view that it seems to me the most beautiful play by Schnitzler. Its lack of conciseness certainly hurts as little as the rambling layout of a precious historical building. And several other factors, the true passion of the love story, the varied colors of the different worlds shown – French émigré aristocracy and Viennese burghers, and in the background the mighty shadow of Napoleon – add to its wonderful, poetic attraction.

None of these and other aspects can be discussed here except those which make *Der junge Medardus* a truly Austrian tragedy. With *Reigen* and *Therese*, this play shares the widest social spectrum of any of Schnitzler's works. Yet the people in *Der junge Medardus* appear not only as representative figures in individual actions like in these other works, they perform also a kind of function as a unit similar to the chorus in the antique tragedy. On the whole this chorus is painted with the same unattractive characteristics which Schnitzler always perceives in the petty bourgeoisie as an entity, but not as individuals. In an uncanny vision of future events in many a country, the people are shown here in their loud hurrah-patriotism and braggadocio at the start of Austria's heroic campaign of 1809. The will to resist ebbs and finally collapses in straight proportion to the rise of danger through enemy action. Submission to the will of the conqueror and even

65

catering to his favors follows on the part of the many. All these seemingly simple sentiments are shown in a variety of nuances ranging from the thoughtless action of the harmless busybody to the undignified, craven curiosity of the habitual loiterer, to the jingo patriotism, brutality, greed, cowardice and cheap rationalizations of the eventual traitor. In the whole literary work of Schnitzler there exists perhaps no more obnoxious and yet true-to-life figure than the merchant of dainty bits Waxhuber, who resembles so much the sublime creation of Helmut Qualtinger's "Herr Karl".[13]

So far this picture would only present the quick change of convictions on the part of the Viennese and their sorry reaction to adversity, an evaluation not any more edifying than that of Austrian politics in *Professor Bernhardi*. The major difference is, however, that here the populace is confronted by the minority of a different brand of Austrian man, centering in the bookdealer's family Klähr, their employee and relative, the saddler Jakob Eschenbacher. One might make the point that this group is socially somewhat above the level of the petty bourgeoisie, though I believe Eschenbacher has been painted as a simple craftsman to make him appear as a more representative character than a bookdealer would have been.[14] He, rather than the somewhat confused and perhaps excessively romantic main character Medardus, is the hero of the play in the true sense of the word. He is a hero after Schnitzler's fashion, and that means a fashion of a particular kind. Quiet, endowed with an ironical kind of humor, sometimes sardonic, and above all sceptical, he sees the world around him without illusions. "Mit dem Patriotismus...halte ich's wie andere mit der Religion. Sie stellen sich fromm und gläubig an, damit die Schwankenden nicht ihren einzigen Halt verlieren." And Eschenbacher adds, "Sind vielleicht die, an denen Gott die meiste Freude hat."[15] And at the time of the outbreak of the war, when enthusiasm and hatred against Napoleon is at its height, he confesses, "Das Grosse zu hassen ist mir nun einmal nicht gegeben, auch wenn ich verspüre, dass es mich vernichten kann. Und die Kleinen zu lieben, will mir nicht gelingen, auch wenn mein Geschick mit dem ihren verbunden ist."[16] True, sentiments of this kind, the sentiments of the ironic and detached "raisonneur" are not rare in Schnitzler's plays. What is rare and indeed unique is, however, the portrayal of the raisonneur not as an intellectual, a wise and mild professor or doctor above the battles of human passion, but as a saddler who dies the sacrificial death of the true hero of the Austrian resistance. It is a sacrifice not born from hatred against the foreign conqueror but from love of country, a feeling to which the saddler, one of Schnitzler's greatest characters gives vent so rarely that it is frequently overlooked.

There is to my knowledge only one other passage where Schnitzler goes beyond this position and expresses similar feelings, not merely in his works but in his life. During the first World War he writes to his friend, the great literary critic Georg Brandes: "Und trotz aller Schwierigkeiten – Miesslichkeiten – Unsicherheiten: wie viel Auftrieb, Stimmungskraft, Talent – welche positive Möglichkeiten in diesem Land, das vielleicht nicht alle seine Bewohner 'Vaterland' aber jeder als 'Heimat' liebt. Ich muss hier innehalten – trotzdem ich dran bin, viel freundlicheres über Österreich zu sagen, als es selbst unsere officiösen Zeitungen zu thun pflegen."[17] When exactly did Schnitzler say this, the Schnitzler who had observed the outbreak and course of the war with the greatest concern, misgivings and sorrow, and without a shred of cheap optimism and loud patriotism? He wrote the letter on August 2, 1918 when the fate of the old empire was doomed and Schnitzler knew this well, indeed presumably better than most of his fellow citizens. There is something of the sentiments, attributed to Cato, in this attitude, "Victrix causa diis placuit, sed victa Catoni." There is something else too. It is the shame which seals Schnitzler's and, through Schnitzler, Eschenbacher's lips to the very last. It is the shame and fear that the most deli-

cate, the most noble feeling may be confounded, through ignorance and ill-will, with the cheap and possibly the opportunistic.

In the evaluation of the Austrian image in Schnitzler's
writings, the expressions of sentiments on this subject must be
weighed and not merely counted. And I believe those voiced
in *Der Junge Medardus* and in Schnitzler's letter to Brahm
carry more weight than any other. Why? The Austrian world
in Schnitzler's life work is only in part moulded by his powerful intellect, his penetrating faculty of observation, his poetic
imagination, and finally his consumate artistic technique. All
this is true enough, but it is not the whole truth. The final and
perhaps supreme element in his great art is here best expressed
in the simple word of Pascal, "The heart has its reasons."

NOTES

[1] Here it should be remembered that the aulic councillor Winkler in
Professor Bernhardi, who represents so to speak the "raisonneur"
in the play and as such the author's view, is pictured as friend and
champion of the Austrian labor movement. It is furthermore generally assumed that Winkler personifies one of Schnitzler's most
respected friends, the former director of the Burgtheater, Max
Burckhard, to whom the play is dedicated. Schnitzler's statements
against politics in the modern sense, particularly in *Der Weg ins
Freie* and in *Buch der Sprüche und Bedenken* (1927) are too numerous
and too well known to be mentioned here. A statement (*ibid.* p. 168)
against Marxism should be taken as evidence of Schnitzler's strong
aversion to any kind of doctrinaire ideology rather than as specific
comment on the labor movement.

[2] Such exceptions would be the prejudiced and opportunistic pro-
fessors in *Professor Bernhardi*. Here, however, their affiliation with
the medical profession is presumably meant to be typical for academic policies rather than medicine. A better and in its way unique
example of a doctor failing as a human being at the bedside of the
dying is Dr. Ferdinand Schmid in the play *Das Vermächtnis*. The
medical status of the insignificant "Dr. Gräsler, Bedearzt" in the
story of the same name seems to me, on the other hand, almost
incidental.

68

[3] See Arthur Schnitzler, *Kritisches. Aus dem Nachlass*, Neue Rundschau, annual 73, issue 2, 3, 1962, pp. 211-13. Observations on Kraus written on June 25, 1912.

[4] The last play in the cycle "Lebendige Stunden".

[5] It is difficult if not impossible to draw a strict dividing line between novels and stories in Schnitzler's prose. While for instance the two masterpieces *Leutnant Gustl* and *Fräulein Else* could be considered as long 'short stories' by virtue of their moderate length, the technique of the inner monologue with its flashback associations unquestionably bursts the frame of the short story or 'Novelle' in its classical sense.

[6] Strangely enough, Schnitzler called *Zwischenspiel* officially a comedy. As his fascinating correspondence with Otto Brahm proves, he himself like the experienced director of the Deutsche Theater in Berlin, Brahm, had grave doubts about the correctness of this nomenclature. See Oskar Seidlin, ed., *Der Briefwechsel Arthur Schnitzler – Otto Brahm*, Berlin, 1953, 140, 143 f., 151 f. Unquestionably Schnitzler's reasoning here was somewhat more complex than that of Professor Seidlin who notes in the introduction to his most creditable edition of the correspondence: "Denn das einzige, was seine zwei grossen 'Komödien', Zwischenspiel und Professor Bernhardi zu Lustspielen macht ist die Tatsache, dass während der drei oder fünf Akte der betreffenden Stücke die Bühne leichenfrei bleibt " Ibid., 23. I would rather think that here, like in *Professor Bernhardi*, Schnitzler wanted to convey the idea that human actions viewed and taken deadly seriously at short range, may in a wider sense evolve into tranquil serenity. This, of course, is not an authoritative interpretation either.

[7] *Der grüne Kakadu*, the first one-act play in a trilogy of the same name, *Letzte Masken*, the third in the cycle "Lebendige Stunden," *Stunde des Erkennens*, the first play in the cycle "Komödie der Worte."

[8] *Der Weg ins Freie*, ed. Berlin, 1922, 219 f.

[9] The actual words are, "Möglich – Da wär ich halt – entschuldigen schon, Herr Professor, – grad so ein Vieh gewesen wie Sie." In view of the strongly Austrian idiomatic character of this sentence the English translation is given in the text.

[10] *Ibid.*, 385 ff.

[11] *Professor Bernhardi*, Act 1. ed. 1913, p. 37.

[12] In *Der Schleier der Beatrice, Die Schwestern*, or *Der Gang zum Weiher*, on the other hand, the historical setting conveys only the atmosphere in a broad way.

69

[13] The character drawn by Helmuth Qualtinger, the author-actor of the Viennese political-cabaret-style revue.

[14] The patriotic German bookdealer, J. P. Palm, executed on Napoleon's direct order in Braunau, Upper Austria, in 1806 presumably was Schnitzler's historical model.

[15] *Der junge Medardus*, Berlin 1910, 2nd act, 1st scene, p. 101.

[16] *Ibid.*, act 1, scene 1, p. 38.

[17] Letter Georg Brandes in Kurt Bergel, ed., *Georg Brandes und Arthur Schnitzler, ein Briefwechsel*, Bern 1956, p. 123.

AN INTERPRETATION OF *DIE WEISSAGUNG*

by Richard H. Lawson

Die Weissagung, hardly the "romantic *Novelle*" that one critic would have it,[1] seems to revolve about a vision experienced
by the young lieutenant Franz von Umprecht under the fixed
gaze of the conjurer Marco Polo. The vision consists of a
moment in Umprecht's future, exactly ten years from the
moment of the vision. Umprecht sees himself on a litter in a
forest clearing, dying, surrounded by wife, son, and daughter,
apparently. Ten years later, or just a few hours short of ten
years, the landowner Umprecht is reading a play, the final
scene of which is identical to the death vision conjured up for
him by Marco Polo. In this play, to be presented in the
evening at his uncle's outdoor theater, Umprecht will enact
the hero.

Having just dined with the author of the play, a guest at
his uncle's villa, Umprecht goes to the playwright's room, tells
his story, and produces a document containing a diagram of
his vision of ten years ago. The playwright, observing that the
diagram coincides with the final scene of his play, moreover
that it contains an extra detail which he had once contemplated for the scene but had abandoned, is strengthened in his
earlier conviction that there existed between him and Umprecht
a "dämonischer Zusammenhang."

71

It will not be surprising if an interpretation of *Die Weis-sagung* is largely Freudian, nor should it at this date be necessary to repeat at any length that this does not imply that Schnitzler's was a derivative talent. In view of Freud's admiration for Schnitzler and his awareness of what Schnitzler was about, his estimate of *Die Weissagung* is unexpectedly curt – that Schnitzler has played a trick on his reader.[2] But Freud may be to some extent right.

The "trick," I would think, consists of the vision, or dream, as Umprecht later calls it. Or rather, the trick consists in the reader's devoting more attention to the vision than to the eloquent reality with which the vision is surrounded, and of which it is at once the echo and the key. For the vision, the dream, is surrounded by a frame of reality, just as the play Umprecht acts in is surrounded by a frame of reality. *Die Weissagung* thus falls within a preferred rubric of Schnitzler's: the play within a play. And it engenders the familiar siren question: what is real? what is illusion? That there is inter-action between the two, we assume. But Schnitzler is not accustomed to mingle the two beyond identification, neither in, for example, *Der grüne Kakadu*, nor in *Die Weissagung*.[3] Let us take his word in delimiting the extent of reality and of illusion, and consider the details, as presented, and their reasonable, often psychological implications.

Umprecht's uncle, the Baron von Schottenegg, is a dilettante sponsor of the arts and artists. His villa lies hidden on the wooded slope of a mountain. No mountain-climbers, the guests at the Baron's villa are drawn mostly from the world of art and from the military. The free composition of this group, we are told, may have caused raised eyebrows in some quarters, but the reputation of the baron and his wife "kept at a distance" any suspicion of immorality.

The art that flourished at the villa was of necessity un-natural, transplanted. Both plays and tableaux were presented. It was through the recall of Umprecht's role in a tableau of the

72

previous year – a monk sitting with his arms propped on a chessboard – that the playwright's memory of Umprecht came to life again. The playwright's memory, or rather forgetfulness concerning the villa, the Baron, and the Baron's nephew Umprecht, is striking enough to warrant a closer inquiry.

The summer before, the Baron prevailed upon the playwright to write a play suited to the unconfined area and natural surroundings of his outdoor theater. The playwright duly submitted the play. The Baron sent his thanks and an invitation to visit during the fall season. At the beginning of September the playwright was at Lake Garda, but he completely forgot that here he was in the immediate vicinity of the Baron's villa: "Ja, mir ist heute, als hätte ich . . . das kleine Schloß und alles dortige Treiben völlig vergessen gehabt." Only on receiving a forwarded letter expressing the Baron's surprise at his continued absence does he make his way to the villa.

He arrives on the day when his play is to be performed. At dinner he sits near Umprecht, and at first he cannot remember him. Then he recalls the tableau of the monk. But he is baffled by Umprecht's actions now. First Umprecht looks at him with sympathy, then with shyness, but always in silence. At a question about last year's tableau, Umprecht becomes embarrassed, and his uncle the Baron answers for him. At his uncle's mention of his nephew's recently discovered acting talent, Umprecht laughs strangely to himself and casts a glance which seems to express a kind of understanding or agreement with the playwright. From this moment on, Umprecht avoids looking at him.

The byplay between Umprecht and the playwright seems on the one hand to pose an enigma and on the other hand to explain it. There is an affinity between the two men—in Schnitzler's words "Sympathie," "Einverständnis," and later, "dämonischer Zusammenhang." Mutal awareness of this connection, I think, accounts as well for Umprecht's alternating encouragement and embarrassment as for the playwright's remarkable forgetfulness about Umprecht, and the place where, and the time when, Umprecht was to be encountered. The specific fear about the connection between Umprecht and himself is probably not the only reason that the playwright forgot the nearness of the Baron's villa and the date of his expected visit there. He has also a general aversion toward gettting involved with the company and the proceedings at the villa, for he says plainly that it was his custom to keep aloof from the other guests.

Umprecht, as we know, seeks out the playwright, because on reading the play, in which he will enact the tragic hero, he discovers that the final scene is the same as that in the vision conjured up for him ten years ago in a bleak Polish cantonment by the Jewish magician Marco Polo. In both, the central figure dies upon a litter. Half a century ago, Reik stated that the "Allmacht der Gedanken" was the key to Umprecht's death as well as to the dramatic anticipation of it by the playwright. Reik named as the possessor of this powerful weapon Marco Polo, who uses it because of the scorn he suffers, as a Jew, from most of the officers in Umprecht's regiment.[4] This of course is true, and certainly the death vision which Marco Polo enables Umprecht to see is the narrative crux of the story. But I also think we should consider Umprecht himself to be playing a more active role in the matter of death wishes. In a word, Umprecht's death wish for himself is central and dominant, those of Marco Polo and the playwright are subordinate.

Why does the playwright, as well as Marco Polo, wish Umprecht dead? The playwright is not a mere unwitting narrative machine, who has accidentally foretold in his play the death of Umprecht.[5] He met Umprecht the previous summer and consciously forgot him. No doubt the latter's habit of sporadic flirting, and the connotation thereof, alienated him into forgetfulness. In his play, which he wrote after his first contact with Umprecht, the subconscious material came to the fore, and the hero of this play finds a sudden death.

74

Umprecht's death wish for himself is not unique. His literary pedigree extends back some years at least. One may think of the Count in Thomas Mann's *Der Tod*, or even of Dostoevsky's Raskolnikov. While I can hardly doubt the narrative existence of Marco Polo, I suggest that his psychological function is like that of the stranger in *Der blinde Geronimo*, in that he serves to embody a recurrent inadmissible wish of the central figure.

The episode of Marco Polo at the cantonment is an analogue of the proceedings at the Baron's villa. In both cases an unnatural, transplanted art is pursued in an artificial environment, on the frontier, isolated, hidden. The artists at the villa are sponsored by a dilettante, the Baron. The artist at the frontier cantonment, Marco Polo, is sponsored by a dilettante of sorts, a prince detailed to the regiment as a major, who seems not to share the anti-Semitism of the other officers. Even a highly particularized geographical reference, such as that to Riva, does double duty, at the villa and at the cantonment.[6] At the Baron's villa are presented not only plays, but also tableaux, *lebende Bilder*. Marco Polo produces something of the same sort, a *lebendes Bild*, when, before conjuring up the vision for Umprecht, he hypnotizes a cadet, who remains standing with arms outstretched for an hour or more, like a man crucified, as Umprecht consistently describes the scene. While the Jew, Marco Polo, wrought this "crucifixion" in retaliation against his tormentors, it is significant that it is Umprecht who gives the deed the deathly name.

Umprecht's reactions in the presence of Marco Polo at the cantonment are like those in the presence of the playwright at the villa, eager but nervous. "Prophezeien Sie mir," he asks the magician. Hardly has Marco Polo grasped his hand when Umprecht apparently feels faint. The lamps begin to flicker, the lines on his hand seem to tremble. Marco Polo knows his man, and, less fearful of himself than is the playwright, he holds Umprecht's hand and leads him outdoors. Then

Umprecht becomes reluctant: "... lassen wir's lieber."
Instead of a mere prophecy, Marco Polo offers to produce a
picture, a vision, perhaps of Umprecht's future wife. This
Umprecht declines, and instead he asks for a picture of himself
ten years in the future. The death vision follows. When it is
over, Marco Polo is smiling, whether painfully or scornfully
Umprecht cannot tell. The terms "Sympathie," "Einverständnis," and above all, "dämonischer Zusammenhang" are
also clearly applicable to the relationship between Umprecht
and Marco Polo.

In the following years Umprecht apparently succeeds to a degree in overcoming what gives evidence of being a latent homosexuality. He marries – his wife's maiden name was Heimsal,
which evokes the idea of *heimliches Schicksal* – has a son, adopts
a daughter, and avoids scenes reminiscent of the death scene
in his vision. But there are many reminders that he cannot in
the long run escape his private fate. His wife one time dyes
her hair red; in his vision a red-headed woman and two
children were kneeling at his death-litter. Umprecht has the
idea, "an Wahnsinn grenzend," of leaving his wife and children, thus escaping the concomitants of his death vision. The
inner component of such an idea must carry with it a deep
sense of guilt. A desire for death, the release from his struggle,
remains, under the conscious surface, just as compelling as it
was in the vision that followed his approaching Marco Polo.

At once a fact as well as an echo of the unforgettable Marco
Polo prophecy, Umprecht on arriving at his uncle's intends to
stay only briefly, and then proceed to — Venice. As a geographical metaphor for homosexuality and death, Venice was of
course most exhaustively employed by Thomas Mann.
Schnitzler's Franz von Umprecht, in saying he is going to
Venice, in effect reiterates the prophecy of death made for him
by the conjurer with a Venetian's name.

The most striking reflection of the playwright's death wish,
and hence Umprecht's, is his play itself, in which Umprecht is

so eager to enact the hero. This hero, seized by a sudden
longing for adventure, deserted his family (cf. Umprecht's
expressed desire). In one day he experienced so much that was
loathsome that he decided to return home. On the way home,
practically on his own doorstep, he is murdered. Dying, he is
unable to explain to his bewildered family either his flight or
his death. (Just as Umprecht has never been able to explain
to his family, nor will he be able to at his death.) However
adept he has become at avoidance, Umprecht's fundamental
wish at last, on the appointed evening, prevails over his
ambivalence.

There remains one apparently mysterious complex in *Die
Weissagung* which becomes clear in the light of the above interpretation and which thereby contributes to it. Umprecht, to
demonstrate to the playwright the identity between his vision
of death and the final scene of the play, produces a notarially
sealed diagram of the former. On the diagram are labeled
figures of the witnesses to his prophesied death, including "man
with raised hands," whom Umprecht further describes as old,
bald, smooth-shaven, with glasses, wearing a green scarf, and
with staring eyes. The playwright is astounded. While such a
figure is not in the final version of his play, he had at one time
contemplated such a figure's rushing across the stage in the
final scene. In the actual presentation of the play, just before
Umprecht's death scene, and death, such a man and such a
scene materialize—the flutist chases his wind-blown wig across
the stage and into the forest, where neither he nor his body is
ever found. Umprecht stares fixedly at this interloper, tries,
just as he has done in the play, to say something, cannot,
sinks back and dies. As to the man who rushes across the
stage, eyes staring like a hypnotist or like a man who sees too
much, arms upraised like a man crucified, we may think that
Umprecht sees his defense shattered again, and definitively,
by a figure that evokes, conceivably represents, the factor of
"dämonischer Zusammenhang."

The playwright kept Umprecht's diagram. The very evening of Umprecht's death, seized by a sudden horror of the Baron's villa, he flees down to Bozen. When on the following day the Baron comes to see him, the playwright tells him Umprecht's story. The Baron can scarcely believe it; the playwright hands him the paper bearing Umprecht's diagram of his vision. But there is no diagram at all. The sheet is blank. For there is no "dämonischer Zusammenhang" between the playwright and the Baron. But there was between Umprecht and the playwright, who like Marco Polo was a catalyst for Umprecht's inadmissible drives and wishes.

NOTES

[1] Allen W. Porterfield, ed. *Stories and Plays*, by Arthur Schnitzler (Boston, 1930), p. xv.

[2] Sigmund Freud, *Complete Psychological Works*, trans. and ed. James Strachey (London, 1955), XVII, 251.

[3] Robert J. Nelson, *Play within a Play* (New Haven, 1958), pp. 119-20.

[4] Theodor Reik, *Arthur Schnitzler als Psycholog* (Minden, Westphalia, 1913), p. 20.

[5] Reik, p. 20, believes the playwright's narcissism demanded that he regard himself as agent of a higher will. I think there is some rationalizing as well.

[6] One of the Baron's guests whom the playwright remembers best is a cavalry officer from Riva, a small resort town on Lake Garda. At the cantonment, before the vision of Umprecht's death, Marco Polo obliquely foretells the colonel's death: "'Von Kälte werden Sie nicht mehr zu leiden haben.' 'Wie,' rief der Oberst aus, 'Kommt unser Regiment also endlich nach Riva?'" In two weeks he is dead.

[7] The blank paper here would also indicate that the vision is not really as basic to Umprecht's situation as he thinks, or as the reader is tempted to think. It is a symptom, not a cause. It seems likely that Umprecht fits himself more and more to the role indicated by the symptomatic vision. On the surface this takes the form of his lately developed acting talent.

ARTHUR SCHNITZLER
UND DER JUNGE HOFMANNSTHAL

Von Walter H. Perl

Es gibt unter den zarten Prologen des jungen Hofmannsthal einen sehr schönen und wenig bekannten zum Dramolett „Der Tor und der Tod," der erstmalig in der Nachlese der Gedichte 1934 abgedruckt worden war. Er stammt aus dem Jahre 1893 und beginnt mit den folgenden Versen:

> In dem alten Wien mit Türmen,
> Mit Basteien, Pagen, Läufern,
> Lebten vier berühmte, grosse
> Gänzlich unbekannte Dichter,
> Hiessen: Baldassar, Ferrante,
> Galeotto und Andrea.
>
> Baldassar war Arzt; er spielte
> Ausserdem auf einem kleinen
> Künstlichen Spinett, aus Noten,
> Spielte süsse Kinderlieder,
> Affectierte Menuette
> Oder ernste Kirchenfugen....

und einige Zeilen weiter heisst es nach der Schilderung von Galeotto und seinem Puppentheater sowie Ferrante und dem semmelblonden Jagdhund Mireio:

... der jüngste
War Andrea: sein Besitztum
War ein grosses, altes dickes
Buch: „die Gesta Romanorum",
Voll der schönsten alten Märchen
Und phantastischer Geschichten,
Voll antiker Anekdoten
Und aristotelscher Weisheit.
Wer dies Buch hat, braucht die Bibel
Braucht Scheheresadens Märchen
Und die heiligen Legenden
Nicht zu lesen, nicht den Platon,
Nicht die Kirchenväter, nicht die
Fabeln des Giovan Boccaccio.
Denn das hat er alles drinnen.
Alle Weisheit, alle Narrheit
Bunt und wundervoll verwoben.

Dies sind Porträts, die der junge Hofmannsthal von Arthur
Schnitzler und sich selbst flüchtig skizzierte; die beiden
andern Dichter sind Richard Beer-Hofmann und Felix Salten.
Der Prolog wird nun fortgeführt:

Diese vier nun waren Freunde,
Und an Sonntagnachmittagen,
Namentlich an jenen lauen
Leuchtenden des Frühlings kamen
Sie zusammen, um zu plaudern.
So geschah es eines stillen
Blauen Sonntagnachmittages,
Dass in Baldassaros Stube
Dieser selbst und Don Ferrante
An dem offnen Fenster lagen
Halbverträumt, indes der gute
Hund Mireio auf dem Pfoten
Seinen Kopf gebettet hatte
Und tiefatmend schlief....

Der Hund träumt, Baldassaro setzt sich ans Klavier und phantasiert in dunklen Mollakkorden. Galeotto und Andrea aber treffen sich in dem alten Haus an der Wollzeile, in dem Beer-Hofmann lebte, kaufen einen Dolch und Rosen und gehen herüber zu Baldassaros Haus, wo Andrea die Rosen durch das Fenster wirft und damit den Besuch ankündigt. Der Prolog endet mit den Versen:

> Roter Kerzen goldne Flammen
> Zündeten die Freunde an und
> Leise las Andrea ihnen
> Eine seltsame gereimte
> Kleine Totentanzkomödie.

Die Datierung ist März/April 1893. Diese zauberhaft leichte dichterische Schilderung einer jener „Lesepremieren," die die vier engen Freunde des „Jungen Wien" besonders liebten, gibt uns Hofmannsthal hier. Beer-Hofmann machte mich in einem Gespräch im Jahre 1932 als erster auf die wirklichen Gestalten dieser kleinen zarten Dichtung aufmerksam. Er besass sie in einer Abschrift von Hofmannsthals Hand und zeigte sie mir, als ich damals lange Gespräche über den jungen Hofmannsthal mit ihm in Wien führte, um Material für meine erste Studie über das lyrische Jugendwerk Hofmannsthals zu sammeln. Hofmannsthal und Arthur Schnitzler waren bereits gestorben. Beer-Hofmann dagegen verschied erst 1945 fast achtzigjährig in New York, nachdem ihn die tragischen Zeitumstände ins amerikanische Exil verschlagen hatten.

Es ist viel über die Gestalt des jungen Hofmannsthal, der sich selbst zu dieser Zeit noch mit dem Pseudonym „Loris" nannte, geschrieben worden. Hermann Bahrs flüchtig skizziertes Porträt aus dem Wiener literarischen Magazin „Die Zeit," später wieder abgedruckt in „Studien zur Kritik der Moderne" (1895) und in der „Freien Bühne" von 1902, ist vielleicht die treffendste Darstellung dieser einmaligen, frühvollendeten Erscheinung; aber ein noch besseres Bild ergeben die Jugend-briefe Hofmannsthals, die zurzeit noch immer nur in den alten Auswahlbänden 1890 bis 1901 und 1900 bis 1910 öffentlich zugänglich sind. Demnächst soll der Briefwechsel Hofmannsthal-Schnitzler erscheinen, der uns teilweise durch das Entgegenkommen des Schnitzler-Archivs an der Universität von Kentucky in Mikrofilmen zugänglich wurde[1]. Dieser Briefwechsel ist ein sicherer Führer durch die Entwicklung dieser einzigartigen literarischen Freundschaft und kann somit als die beste Quelle für die von uns darzustellenden Beziehungen dienen. Das Material könnte nur noch durch die sehnlichst erwarteten Tagebücher Schnitzlers weiter ergänzt werden. Der erste Teil dieser Tagebücher, die von Schnitzler selbst mit einer wohl vierzigjährigen Sekretierungsbestimmung versehen wurden, könnte in der Tat schon heute der Oeffentlichkeit zugänglich gemacht werden, etwa von der Frühzeit bis zum Jahre 1910, wie auch seine der gleichen Frühzeit entstammende Autobiographie. Gerade hier könnte die kürzlich ins Leben gerufene Internationale Arthur Schnitzler-Forschungsgesellschaft ein weites Betätigungsfeld finden. Hofmannsthal schreibt im Jahre 1903 einmal an Schnitzler:

> Fast beneide ich diejenigen, die nach uns einmal
> in Ihren ausführlichen Tagebüchern lesen und
> wochenlang darin leben werden – wie es mir jetzt
> mit dem prachtvollen Briefwechsel Hebbels geht...

Der literarische Durchbruch des jungen Hofmannsthal, der seit seinem dreizehnten Lebensjahr Verse geschrieben hatte, geschah im Frühjahr 1891, und das ist die gleiche Zeit, in der er Arthur Schnitzler, den damals etwa dreissigjährigen Dichter und Arzt, kennen lernte. Er wurde als Siebzehnjähriger von dem über zwölf Jahre älteren Freund als ebenbürtig, wenn nicht sogar als überlegen aufgenommen. Es ist hier nicht unsere Absicht, die Einzelheiten dieser Freundschaft, die sich in dem angekündigten Briefwechsel widerspiegeln wird, im Detail nachzuzeichnen, sondern wir wollen aus den vorhandenen Zeugnissen die wesentlichen Schlüsse für die menschlichen und literarischen Beziehungen beider Dichter ziehen. Die Freundschaft, im ganzen gesehen, ist immer bestimmt durch literatische Anerkennung und gegenseitige Hochschätzung, selbst da, wo sie gelegentlich in freundliche Scherze hineingleitet.

Während Hofmannsthal in einer Reihe von anderen Briefwechseln, vor allem mit den gleichaltrigen Freunden, stärker persönlich hervortritt, wie z. B. in der Korrespondenz mit Leopold von Andrian, die gleichfalls in absehbarer Zeit veröffentlicht werden soll, oder in den ergreifenden Briefen an Georg von Franckenstein, so bleibt die Freundschaft mit dem eine halbe Generation älteren Schnitzler etwa auf der gleichen Ebene wie die mit Beer-Hofmann oder Hermann Bahr. Es gibt einen ständigen Gedankenaustausch, ein sehr feines Verständnis für künstlerische Werte, eine wohlwollende, aber zugleich bewusst kritische Anerkennung des gegenseitigen Werkes, aber auf der andern Seite ein absolutes Verhüllen der persönlichen Sphäre. Hofmannsthal schreibt darüber einmal von einer Waffenübung in einem Brief von Tlumacz in Galizien aus dem Jahre 1896, nachdem sie einander bereits mehr als fünf Jahre kannten:

> Die ganze Zeit, seit wir uns kennen, ist mir als ein Ganzes eingefallen, wie eine Landschaft, aber viel merkwürdiger... Mir ist eingefallen wie mir G (entweder Goldmann oder Gustav Schwarzkopf) zum ersten Mal von Nietzsche und Bahr erzählt hat, das kleine Redactionszimmer und unsere ersten Begegnungen, und alles das kommt mir so unglaublich vergangen vor, und so nett und altmodisch wie eine Geschichte aus der Jean Paul Zeit. Wir haben doch in diesen paar Jahren sehr viele schöne Stunden gehabt. Wir haben sehr oft das Leben gross und reich gesehen und waren imstande, viele Dinge

aufeinander zu beziehen und immer hat sich's ver-
ändert, das war das Schönste. Auch dass wir nicht
zuviel voneinander wissen und immer jeder wie ein
neuer aus seinem Leben hervortritt und wieder hin-
eingeht, ist sehr schön.

Diese Sätze könnten gleichsam wie ein Leitgedanke über dieser
Lebensfreundschaft stehen, die sich über mehr als achtund-
dreissig Jahre bis zu Hofmannsthals vorzeitigem Tode hin
erstreckte – auch wenn sie in späteren Jahren durch die
eigenen Lebensschicksale der Dichter, vor allem Heirat und
Familiengründung, wie auch durch Werk und Beruf sich
stärker distanzierte.

Wie begann diese Freundschaft? Genaue Aufzeichnungen
über das erste Zusammentreffen sind uns bislang nicht bekannt geworden, sie mögen vielleicht später einmal bei der
Eröffnung der Schnitzlerschen Tagebücher auftauchen. Die
ersten Briefzeugnisse vom Frühjahr und Sommer 1891
sprechen dafür, dass irgendein literarischer Freund, wahrscheinlich der Romanschriftsteller Gustav Schwarzkopf, den
jungen Hofmannsthal, der um diese Zeit noch zur Schule ging
und daher sein erstes Dramolett „Gestern” unter dem Pseudonym Theophil Morren veröffentlichte – Gymnasialschülern
war die Publikation von Druckschriften nicht erlaubt –, mit
dem älteren Schnitzler bekannt gemacht haben muss. Wir kennen Postkarten mit Stempeldaten vom 18. Januar 1891 und
eine andere mit Hermann Bahrs Adressenangabe vom 14.
Februar 1891. Ausserdem gibt es im ersten Hofmannsthal-
Briefauswahlband einen undatierten Frühbrief, der der Beginn der eigentlichen Korrespondenz zu sein scheint. Er
lautet:

> Geschätzter Herr, Dienstag um 12 Uhr bin ich
> sehr natürlich in der Schule, dann mache ich Aufga-
> ben, und von 3-4 habe ich Deutschstunde. Aber
> Mittwoch um 1/2 1 möchte ich ins Hotel Kummer

84

kommen können. Wenn Sie aber nicht mehr antworten, betrachte ich diesen Antrag als abgelehnt
und komme erst Freitag zu Beraton[2] sitzen.

Diese Mitteilung ist noch mit grosser Distanziertheit geschrieben, aber seit dem Sommer 1891 ist dann die Anrede
„Lieber Arthur" selbstverständlich. Zu einem „Du" ist es bei
den Dichtern zeitlebens nie gekommen. Für ihre häufigen
Zusammenkünfte haben wir ein anderes Briefzeugnis aus dem
Jahre 1891. Hofmannsthal schreibt da an Hermann Bahr
(undatiert):

> Ich möchte Ihnen gerne das Sonntagrendez-
> vous geben, gehe aber nach dem Lunch ins Philhar-
> monische Konzert. Zwischen 4 und 6 Uhr aber bin
> ich bei Dr. Schnitzler, Kärntnerring 12, 3. Stock.
> Wenn Sie dorthin kämen, würden Sie ihm und mir
> eine aufrichtige Freude machen. Man sitzt und
> plaudert besser wie im Kaffeehaus und ist ebenso
> allein, ungestörter als bei Griensteidl. Die Lampen
> haben rote Schirme. Es gibt Kognac, man ist nicht
> zu Gast und es gibt keine Hausfrau. Am Schreib-
> tisch liegen Bahr, Barrès, Barbey d'Aurevilly und
> noch anderes, das alliteriert. Es riecht nach der
> Boheme von Wien 1891 – Paris 1840, wie sie so
> hübsch im Märchen ist ...

Literarische Pläne werden im frühen Briefwechsel diskutiert.
Da schreibt Schnitzler einmal im Juli 1892 auf eine Mitteilung
Hofmannsthals hin:

> Was macht Ihr Stück? Es wundert mich, dass
> Sie zugleich einen 2ten und 5ten Akt schreiben
> können, so sicher bin ich mit meinen Gestalten nie.
> Es kann Ihnen doch im 3ten Akt was einfallen
> oder gar passieren, wovon ich im 2ten noch nichts
> rechtes weiss. Selbst wenn eine genaue Skizze vor-

liegt, wage ich es nicht und habe keine Lust dazu.
Ich will mit ihnen (den Gestalten) weiterleben, und
Gedanke für Gedanke und Tat für Tat, wie sie selber. Ich darf manches vorausahnen, aber wissen
darf ich es nicht.

Gleich zu Beginn der Freundschaft steht ein gemeinsames
Unternehmen, nämlich die Drucklegung des „Anatol" in der
ersten Buchfassung von 1892, der zu Hofmannsthal seinen
schönen Prolog beisteuert. Seit dem Frühjahr 1892 wird dieser
Druck in Briefen diskutiert, und Schnitzler fragt an, ob
Hofmannsthal dem Prolog irgendeinen besonderen Namen
geben will; gezeichnet wird er auf Hofmannsthals Wunsch nur
mit „Loris". Schnitzler schreibt im Herbst 1892 kurz vor der
Drucklegung:

> Ihr Gedicht leitet die Sammlung ein. Wollen Sie
> ihm irgendeinen Namen geben; haben Sie sonst
> noch irgendwelchen Wunsch? Möchten Sie im In-
> halt verzeichnet sein? In ein paar Tagen beginnt die
> Drucklegung. Haben Sie schon bemerkt, wie mise-
> rabel „Agonie" ist? Gut ist nur die „Frage an das
> Schicksal" und „Episode".

Dieser Prolog nun fand sich unter dem Briefmaterial auf
Mikrofilmen in einer Abschrift von Hofmannsthals Hand, und
er ist dort mit „Theophil Morren," dem früheren Pseudonym
das Hofmannsthal benutzte, unterschrieben. Die Frage muss
zumindest erwogen werden ob der Prolog ursprünglich für
den „Anatol" gedichtet worden war, oder ob er nur die allgemeine Stimmung der Wiener Amateurtheateraufführungen
der Zeit widerspiegelte und dann dem „Anatol" für den Druck
beigegeben wurde.

Vergleicht man nämlich Prolog und Werk, so ergibt sich
zunächst kaum eine innere Verbindung. Der Prolog, in dem
von Heine übernommenen Kurzvers, beschreibt in der Tat

eigentlich nur das „Wien des Canaletto" von 1760 in einer Technik, die wohl von Watteau und dem französischen Rokoko beeinflusst scheint, zugleich aber auch impressionistisch mit Lichtreflexen, Farben und Tönen arbeitet. Lediglich die berühmten Endverse stehen in einer gewissen Beziehung zur Stimmung der Schnitzlerschen Szenenfolge:

> Also spielen wir Theater,
> Spielen unsre eignen Stücke,
> Frühgereift und zart und traurig,
> Die Komödie unsrer Seele,
> Unsres Fühlens Heut und Gestern,
> Böser Dinge hübsche Formel,
> Glatte Worte, bunte Bilder,
> Halbes, heimliches Empfinden,
> Agonien, Episoden ...

Im „Anatol" sind bekanntlich zwei Szenen unter dem Titel „Agonie" und „Episode" vorhanden, und „Gestern" könnte eine Anspielung auf Hofmannsthals erstes Stück sein. Aber daran schliesst sich wieder das ganz impressionistisch gesehene allgemeine Schlussbild an:

> Manche hören zu, nicht alle ...
> Manche träumen, manche lachen,
> Manche essen Eis ... und manche
> Sprechen sehr galante Dinge ...
> ... Nelken wiegen sich im Winde,
> Hochgestielte, weisse Nelken,
> Wie ein Schwarm von weissen Faltern,
> Und ein Bologneserhündchen
> Bellt verwundert einen Pfau an.

Hieran schliesst sich dann die bunte Szenenfolge des „Anatol," immer in einem klugen und geistreich psychologischen Dialog gehalten, zugleich auch immer leicht mit dem erotischen Element spielend. Junge Männer, Frauen und Mädchen der

Zeit um 1892 sind hier vom scharfsichtigen Psychologen Schnitzler treffend skizziert, zugleich mit einer aphoristisch belebten Sprache, die an die fast gleichzeitige elegante Dialogführung Oscar Wildes erinnert. Sicherlich ist „Anatol" das graziöseste, heiterste und in gewissem Sinne am stärksten spielerische Werk des sonst oft so tragischen Psychologen. So wurde es ein klassisches Bühnenwerk, das bis heute nichts von seiner Frische eingebüsst hat und selbst noch in englischer Übertragung eine starke Wirkung ausübt. (Freilich darf man es nicht als ein „Broadway-Musical" nach dem Fair Lady Rezept auffrisieren, wie es kürzlich in New York geschah.)

In der Divergenz der Szenenfolge und des Hofmannsthalschen Prologes liegt nun der ganze Gegensatz der beiden individuellen künstlerischen Ausdrucksformen. Trotz grösster menschlicher Wertschätzung, sowohl im Persönlichen wie im Künstlerischen, sind die beiden Dichter in ihrem Schaffen diametral entgegengesetzt. Hofmannsthal ist in der Frühzeit vorwiegend ein lyrischer Dichter, und selbst seine Dramolette („Gestern," „Der Tod des Tizian," „Der Tor und der Tod") sind lyrische Dramen, lyrische Gestaltungen sogar im Dialog bei einer seltenen Frühvollendung des dichterischen Ausdrucks aber sie haben nichts mit der Gesellschaftsschilderung der gleichzeitigen Schnitzlerschen Dramen gemeinsam. Erst viel später gleichen sich die Arbeitsweisen beider Dichter einander an; lange nach der Jahrhundertwende schreibt Hofmannsthal Prosakomödien wie auch Dramen („Sylvia im Stern," „Der Schwierige"), während sich Schnitzler schon vorher gelegentlich in Versdramen („Paracelsus," „Der Schleier der Beatrice," später „Casanova in Spa") versucht hatte. Aber künstlerische Gegensätze bieten oft bei ganz verschiedener Ausdrucksform und Arbeitstechnik eine ausgezeichnete Grundlage für positive und freundschaftliche Kritik, und so ist denn auch der Briefwechsel recht oft den neuen Werken, der Arbeitsweise und der Beurteilung des persönlichen Schaffens gewidmet. Unter allen Freunden Hofmannsthals ist Schnitzler sicherlich derjenige

mit dem klarsten künstlerischen Urteil, viel klarer als der oft
verschwommen mystisierende Hermann Bahr oder der stark
subjektive und oft ein wenig zu sensitive Leopold von Andrian.
Hofmannsthal wendet sich an Schnitzler, wenn er künstlerischen Rat und Hilfe braucht. Aber anderseits legt auch
Schnitzler viel Wert auf das Urteil des Jüngeren. So schreibt
Hofmannsthal einmal am 1. Februar 1893:

> Ich denke oft an die Novelle vom „Sterben" und
> möchte viel mehr davon reden als geschieht. Sie
> haben was gegen die Geschichte, wenigstens schei-
> nen Sie sie totschweigen zu wollen.

Wohl zu den interessantesten Briefzeugnissen dieser gegenseitigen Kritik gehört eine Stelle aus einem Brief Schnitzlers
vom 26. November 1855 auf Grund der Lektüre von Hofmannsthals „Märchen der 672sten Nacht." Da schreibt Schnitzler:

> Eben habe ich den Kaufmannssohn gelesen.
> Folgendes find ich: Die Geschichte hat nichts von
> der Wärme und dem Glanz eines Märchens, wohl
> aber in wunderbarer Weise das fahle Licht des
> Traums, dessen rätselhafte wie verwischte Ueber-
> gänge und das eigene Gemisch von Deutlichkeit
> der geringen und Blässe der besonderen Dinge, das
> eben dem Traum zukommt. Sobald ich mir die Er-
> lebnisse des Kaufmannssohnes als Traum vorstelle,
> werden Sie mir höchst ergreifend; denn es gibt
> solche Träume, sie sind eigentlich auch Schicksale
> und man könnte gut verstehen, dass sich Menschen
> die von solchen Träumen geplagt werden, aus Ver-
> zweiflung umbringen.

> Auch ist nicht zu vergessen: Die Empfindungen
> des Kaufmannssohns sind wie im Traum geschildert,
> die unsägliche Unheimlichkeit, die irgendein Kinder-

gesicht, eine Tür für einen annehmen kann, wenn man sie träumt, finden kaum im wachen Leben ein Analogon. Ihre tiefste Bedeutung verliert die Geschichte durchaus nicht, wenn der Kaufmannssohn aus ihr erwacht, statt an ihr zu sterben. Ich würde ihn sogar mehr beklagen, denn das Tödliche fühlen wir besser als den Tod. Ich will mit alledem nicht sagen, dass mir nicht auch ein Märchen des gleichen Inhalts, *ganz* desselben recht wäre; aber Sie haben die Geschichte sicher als Traum erzählt – erinnere ich mich jetzt zurück; so sehe ich den Kaufmannssohn im Bett stöhnend sich wälzen und er tut mir sehr leid...

Hier wird der Psychologe Schnitzler zum kritisch beratenden Freund. Aber er spricht auch ebenso offen von sich und seinen Stücken. So heisst es einmal in einem Brief vom 2. August 1893:

Ich hab mir aus meinen kleinen Schmerzen die grossen Dreiakter machen können und seit meinen grossen Schmerzen werden mir nur die kleinen Novellen gelingen. Was ich zunächst schreiben werde, ist unklar, am liebsten eins meiner umrissfertigen Stücke, aber ich stehe der dramatischen Kunst unglaublich mutlos gegenüber, ja ich habe in der letzten Zeit oft die Empfindung, dass ich überhaupt nie ein gutes Stück werde schreiben können. Gestalten und Szenen, einzelne wären da; aber mir ist jedes strategische Talent verloren. Vielleicht hatte ich es auch nie.

Auch Hofmannsthal ist in der gleichen Zeit ähnlich offen und selbstkritisch; er schreibt kurz zuvor am 19. Juli 1893:

... ich habe mir sehr viel abzugewöhnen, aber es sind wenigstens lauter echte Dichterkrankheiten. Mir scheint dieser Satz klingt masslos arrogant.

90

Ausser den Besuchen und Lesepremièren ist die gemeinsame Zeit beider Dichter und ihrer Freunde etwa bis zu ihrer Heirat mit vielen Ausflügen in die Wiener Umgebung, oft mit Radtouren und später mit gemeinsamen Reisen, vor allem in die Südtiroler Landschaft und nach Italien, ausgefüllt. Dennoch bleibt, wie schon anfangs erwähnt, immer ein gewisser Abstand im Persönlichen bestehen, der nur überwunden wird, wenn wirkliche Schicksalsschläge wie der Tod von nahen Freunden oder Angehörigen den Gesprächspartner treffen; dann allerdings sprechen beide mit einem seltenen Zartgefühl. All das bezieht sich auf die erste Periode ihrer Freundschaft, etwa auf die Jahre von 1891 bis 1901, so lange, bis die beiden Dichter fast um die gleiche Zeit heiraten. An sich waren ihre Frauen dem literarischen Freundeskreis schon lange vorher bekannt, vor allem Gerty Schlesinger, Hofmannsthals Gattin, die oft mit Schnitzler und Bahr Rad gefahren war, aber auch die Schauspielerin Olga wird ein gutes Bindeglied, und es sind dann nach 1901 vor allem die Frauen, die die Freundschaft weiter am Leben erhalten. Dennoch kommen die Dichter auch ab und zu allein zu Aussprachen zusammen, und Schnitzler hat ihr menschliches Verhältnis zueinander noch so spät wie 1914 sehr klar in einem Brief ausgedrückt; er schreibt da an Hofmannsthal:

... denn ich glaube, Sie haben das Bedürfnis, mir von Ihrer neuen Arbeit was zu erzählen – und ich rechne, wie Ihnen nicht unbekannt ist, zu meinen besten Stunden, wenn Sie sich zu mir über Ihre Sachen aussprechen. Und aus solchen Stunden scheiden wir, wie Sie wohl schon oft gefühlt haben, so im besten Sinne verbunden, dass ein Auseinanderlaufen äusserer Lebenslinien für das Wesentliche unserer Beziehungen auf längere Zeit hin ohne Bedeutung, wenn auch oft mit einiger Wehmut zu empfinden bleibt. Im Ganzen aber glaube ich trotz aller Ehrfurcht vor dem Gesetz der Entwicklung, immer mehr an die Constanz der menschlichen Beziehungen, sowie an die der Menschen. Was aus uns und anderen wird, hat Ahnung längst vorausempfunden und jeder Wolkendunst unserer Jugend, der sich harmlos zu verziehen schien, kommt irgendwann einmal als Gewitter wieder. Von diesem Ausflug ins Allgemeinere oder Halbwahre, kehre ich gern in die Realität wieder, so wie ich Sie sehr bald, und wie ich hoffe, in besserer Stimmung als Ihr Brief mir vertraute, zu sehen und sprechen wünsche.   Herzlichst Ihr Arthur.

Gelegentlich kommt es allerdings auch zu kritischen Augenblicken in der Freundschaft, wie etwa bei der Ablehnung, die Schnitzlers Roman „Der Weg ins Freie" durch Hofmannsthal erfuhr. In der Tat ist „Der Weg ins Feie" wahrscheinlich eins der unglücklichsten und am wenigsten einheitlichen Werke Schnitzlers. Er ist auf weite Strecken hin ein Schlüsselroman der Wiener Gesellschaft um 1900, in dem Judenfrage, Kunst, Musik, freie Liebe und Politik bunt durcheinander spielen. Ausserdem enthält er zahlreiche Porträts und Skizzen von Freunden und Bekannten beider Dichter, zum Teil sogar von sehr nahestehenden Freunden Hofmannsthals, wie die der beiden Barone Franckenstein, Clemens', des Musikers und späteren Intendanten, der im Roman den Namen Georg von Wergenthin trägt, und Georgs, des Diplomaten und späteren österreichischen Gesandten in Londen, den der Dichter hier Felicien nennt. Auch Schnitzler selbst und einige seiner eigenen Schicksalsschläge sind sehr eindeutig in der Gestalt des Dichters Heinrich Bermann zu finden, wobei sogar der Selbstmord einer Freundin, die sich aus unglücklicher Liebe zum Dichter umbrachte, nicht ausgelassen wird. Es gibt zahlreiche Porträts von Beer-Hofmann, Salten und anderen Zeitgestalten in diesem Roman, und wir glauben nicht fehlzugehen, wenn selbst der Salon Schlesinger und der Salon

Friedmann, die die massgebenden literarischen Zentren im Wiener Kreis waren, in irgendeiner halbverdeckten Form gezeichnet sind, so dass sogar ein Porträt von Hofmannsthals Frau zu finden zu sein scheint. Es ist kein Wunder, dass dieses Werk Hofmannsthal, der besonders im Persönlichen von ausserordentlichem Feingefühl war, höchst peinlich sein musste, wenngleich der Roman inhaltlich wohl acht bis zehn Jahre vor der Niederschrift spielt; so antwortet er zunächst überhaupt nicht auf den Roman und teilt Schnitzler nur mit, dass ihn dieser Roman verstöre und er daher lieber nicht seine Meinung über das Buch schriebe. Schnitzler antwortet darauf in einem Brief vom 6. August 1908 aus Seis am Schlern:

> ... dass Sie zu meinem Roman kein glückliches Verhältnis gefunden haben, war in der Tat nicht schwer zu merken, und so sehr ich Ihrem Ausspruch beistimme, dass Sie zwischen mir und meinen Arbeiten keine Grenze ziehen können, ich empfinde ihn als doppelt und zehnfach gegenüber einem Werk, das mich in Gedanken und Ausführung durch manches reife und höchst bewusste Jahr meines Lebens vornehmlich beschäftigt hat. Aber es erweist sich doch, was Sie selbst zu spüren scheinen, wie es kaum denkbar ist, zum Dichter eines Werkes, das für eine ganze Entwicklungsperiode dieses Dichters bedeutend ist, in einem glücklicheren Verhältnis zu stehen als zu der Dichtung selbst und das ich Ihnen für den Takt dankbar bin, der Sie richtig erkennen liess, jedes weitere Wort über ein Werk zu unterlassen, das nichts vermochte als Sie zu verstören, und von dem mir ein unverlierbar und untrüglich starkes Nachgefühl in der Seele geblieben ist ...

Diese letzte Frage führt uns dazu, zu prüfen, ob auch Hofmannsthals Gestalt und Persönlichkeit irgendwie in Schnitzlers Dichtung eingedrungen ist. Er selbst hat wohl auf Grund eines Gesprächs mit Schnitzler in einem Brief von 1907 darauf hingewiesen, dass in gewissem Sinne Stefan von Sala im Drama „Der einsame Weg" Züge von ihm trägt. Dieses Stück liebte Hofmannsthal im Gegensatz zu manchem anderen von Schnitzler ausserordentlich, wie er es in einem Brief vom 13. November 1903 ausdrückt, den er mit den Worten abschliesst: „Ich bin sehr glücklich, dass Sie, lieber Arthur, etwas so Schönes, so Tiefes, mit nichts Vergleichbarem machen konnten."

Zusammenfassend lässt sich über die Beziehungen zwischen Schnitzler und Hofmannsthal sagen, dass die Freundschaft der beiden Dichter vor allem in den wichtigen Jahren von 1891 bis 1901 wohl eine der wesentlichsten für Hofmannsthal war, aber auch für Schnitzler vor allem im literarischen Sinne viel bedeutete und so beiden Dichtern unendlich viel gegeben hat. Gerade bei so verschiedenen künstlerischen Anlagen war die kritisch-objektive Erfassung des Gesprächspartners von allergrössstem Wert und hat dazu beigetragen, dass sich das Werk beider Dichter reicher und vollkommener entfalten konnte. In einer Zeit, in der die Tagespresse sowohl Schnitzlers als auch Hofmannsthals Werk angriff und verunglimpfte,[3] haben beide klar erkannt, dass ihre Kunst weit über dem Alltag stand und zu dem gerechnet werden muss, was heute in unserer Wertung fünfzig oder mehr Jahre nach der Entstehung als wahrhafte Dichtung bestehen bleibt.

ANMERKUNGEN

[1] Die folgenden Zitate aus dem Briefwechsel zwischen Schnitzler und Hofmannsthal werden mit freundlicher Erlaubnis des S. Fischer-Verlags, Frankfurt am Main, wiedergegeben.

[2] Beraton war ein zu dieser Zeit in Wien lebender Bildhauer.

[3] Brief Hofmannsthal vom 23. März 1899 aus Berlin: „Hier sind meine armen Stücke von einer beispiellosen Presse erschlagen worden und mussten nach dem dritten Mal abgesetzt werden."

NIETZSCHE AND SCHNITZLER

by Herbert W. Reichert

To confront Friedrich Nietzsche and Arthur Schnitzler, with a
view to ascertaining whether the former influenced the latter,
may seem to some readers a strained and far-fetched pro-
cedure, so that it is perhaps well to explain why the effort was
made. The present investigation does not stand isolated but
is part of a larger inquiry concerning the extent of Nietzsche's
influence on modern German writers in general. Since many
of the eminent writers of Schnitzler's generation and the generation which followed him experienced the impact of Nietzsche
– Hauptmann, Hesse, Musil, George, Rilke, Wedekind,
Sternheim, Kaiser, Heinrich and Thomas Mann, to name a
few – ,we were curious whether Schnitzler, too, had been
caught up in the powerful tide of Nietzschean ideas.

Contrary to the other Nietzsche-influence studies that we
had previously made, there was initially very little to go on to
indicate a possible tie between Nietzsche and Schnitzler.
However, some encouraging facts were immediately evident.
We knew, for example, as does every interested scholar, that
the apparent contrast between the two men was not as great
as it might at first seem to be. Schnitzler, despite his air of
worldly sophistication and apparent fascination with the theme
of erotic love, despite his normal family life, his circle of

friends, his cycling tours and tennis-playing, was anything but a jovial extrovert. In the midst of his friends he remained withdrawn. At the core of his mundane dramas, he constantly probed the basic questions of man's nature and destiny. Like the sage of Sils-Maria, Schnitzler was essentially a lonely and melancholy thinker brooding over the futility of life. Like the former, he became increasingly bitter as a result af an unceasing barrage of vindictive criticism, venting his wrath in caustic aphorisms. To a certain extent, Schnitzler even shared with Nietzsche the isolation and pessimism brought on by physical suffering, as Schnitzler experienced in middle-age an ear malady that caused increasing deafness and an unpleasant and constant ringing in his ears.

Even more intriguing than the similarities in their personalities and lives is the affinity in their outlooks. Schnitzler was dubious as to the possibility of ascertaining truth. He distrusted philosophical systems and held them to be beautiful, artistic creations. Ideals existed for the most part in the mind of man alone. The path of life wove its tortuous way through an almost impenetrable network of illusions. Whoever saw to the core of life, through the glittering lure of fame and "weite Welt," faced only bleak disillusionment. There was only one great and terrible and incomprehensible reality: death. For Schnitzler, reality was encompassed in the three words: illusion, mortality, futility. And we venture to say despite his dedication to the life of the physician and artist, that Schnitzler agreed basically with his protagonist, Friedrich Hofreiter, that love alone made the futile game worthwhile.

Such nihilism and cognitive subjectivism are generally considered as belonging to the great contributions of Nietzsche to our time. Hence it seemed particularly interesting to attempt to determine to what degree Schnitzler's position was a result of his own cogitations as a psychologist or – if one will – psychoanalyst with a metaphysical bent, and to what degree it may have been brought about by reading Nietzsche. In this connection, it is pertinent to note that the only other modern German dramatist to utilize illusion and ironic reversal of values in his plays to the extent that Schnitzler did, Georg Kaiser, stood deeply in Nietzsche's debt.

Schnitzler shared with Nietzsche also his contempt for conventional morality; from first to last the dramatist mocked the superficiality and hypocrisy of the bourgeois way of life. However, their views differ somewhat with regard to the notion of ethical responsibility. The ideal of the superman implies a considerable degree of voluntarism and a highly subjective ethics; it will be remembered that although the superman was to heed instinct, he was not simply to yield to desire. In fact, to be true to himself, to develop his potentialities to the full, he had to overcome desire. *Selbstüberwindung* and consequently, voluntarism, were key concepts for Nietzsche. It must also be kept in mind that keeping faith with oneself in Nietzsche's sense differed in its complete subjectivism from the idea of a natural law of mankind as expounded by Schiller and Keller; Nietzsche insisted that the superman pursue his course with ruthless self-interest, disregarding pity and all conventional notions of good and evil.

Schnitzler's characters, on the other hand, often had little free-will; they lived in a world of dreams and illusions and were frequently controlled by their emotions. Even his most voluntaristic protagonists appear puppets in the hands of an all-powerful fate. Helene, in *Der junge Medardus*, for example, professes to believe only in the strong assertion of will:

> Es gibt kein Glück, es gibt nur den Willen, das
> Schicksal zu zwingen. Es gibt keine Freunde, nur
> den Willen über Menschen Herr zu sein. Der Wille
> ist alles.[1]

Yet she yields despite herself to the impulse of love and her courageous plans are thwarted by tragic misunderstanding. Her lover, Medardus, was also initially a defiant voluntarist, but he, too, falls victim to his feelings and tragic coincidence, so that ultimately his freedom is restricted to dying a meaningless death in defiance of Napoleon.

With regard to the matter of subjective ethics, Schnitzler apparently concurred in the idea but did not go as far as Nietzsche. Schnitzler's favorite protagonist is an egocentric artist-type, akin to the superman, who knows no law other than his own self-interest. However, this protagonist seldom stands alone, but is confronted by some person imbued with restraint and common sense, usually a doctor, who holds to an enlightened but objective standard of morality. One can trace the former type from Anatol and the latter from Max. Often the two are friends, and rarely does the doctor-type condemn his amoral friend, as the doctor is not at all sure that man possesses the wisdom or freedom to act differently than he does. It is important to note that Schnitzler's attitude as revealed in the plays and narratives seems to go a step farther than the tolerance of the doctor, and often we sense a deep if veiled sympathy with the amoral artist.

It will be seen from the foregoing, and the problem will be taken up again later on, that, whereas Schnitzler's and Nietzsche's ethical positions were not identical, they have important points in common. And inasmuch as many writers of the time received demonstrable inspiration from Nietzsche's violently anti-bourgeois code, it is conceivable that Schnitzler was similarly affected.

To my knowledge, no one has yet sought to demonstrate the possibility that Nietzsche helped to mold some of Schnitzler's ideas. However, one scholar regards Schnitzler as carrying on the tradition of Nietzsche; Kurt Bergel's final words in this regard, written in 1956, read as follows:

> Diese Analyse des Seelischen dient der Wahrheit
> und darin ist Schnitzler, wie man noch nie erkannt
> zu haben scheint, der Nachfolger Nietzsches.[2]

98

So much by way of introduction. The first bit of evidence we uncovered that gave hint of a possible direct tie between Nietzsche and Schnitzler was the fact that the dramatist had for long years, from 1894-1927 been on the best of terms with the Danish critic, Georg Brandes. It will be recalled that Brandes was the person who had first realized the significance of Nietzsche for his times and had first popularized him in Europe. Although himself far too individualistic to be considered a disciple of Nietzsche, Brandes sincerely admired the radical liberalism inherent in Nietzsche's doctrine. Had Schnitzler been hostile to Nietzsche's views, it is not likely that his friendship for Brandes would have remained so firm throughout the years and that the correspondence would have remained free of conflicts of opinion.[3] However, this evidence has, admittedly, only limited significance, since the correspondence makes no mention of Nietzsche. In the systematic investigation of Schnitzler's principal works that we now undertook, our hopes dwindled from work to work; possible Nietzschean motifs cropped up here and there, but no specific references to Nietzsche, no clearly defined Nietzschean ideas were discernible.

It was only toward the end of our reading that we achieved a *Durchbruch*, as the Germans would say, in perusing *Der Weg ins Freie*, a rather slim but not unmeaningful break-through.

Der Weg ins Freie, it will be recalled, is one of the most sincere and most personal of Schnitzler's works. Many superficial similarities between its hero, Georg Wergenthin and Schnitzler may be noted. For example, Georg lived with an older brother, of whom he was fond, in an apartment with a fine view of the Ringstrasse in Vienna; one passage in which Georg is looking out over the city from his balcony on a summer evening seems a veritable paraphrase of part of a letter Schnitzler wrote to Otto Brahm on August 2, 1904[4]. Georg liked to cycle in the Vienna woods just as Schnitzler did; and many similar parallels might be cited. Then, Georg was another Anatol, a typical Schnitzler hero, sophisticated, artistic, sensitive and sensual, slightly dilettantish and a little lazy, uncertain of himself and his true desires, in whose heart truth and deception existed side by side. One may argue that Georg was not Schnitzler himself but only a typical protagonist.[5] We are wont in this connection to think of the many similar characters that Goethe created after the Sesenheim episode. Of course Georg does not represent the whole Schnitzler. Two souls seem to have dwelled in Schnitzler's breast as well, both Max and Anatol; or in this case, Georg on the one hand, and Heinrich Bergmann and old Dr. Stauber on the other.

In *Der Weg ins Freie*, Schnitzler makes several references to Nietzsche in the course of the narrative, and we believe a careful analysis of these references can reveal his opinion of the latter as a moralist.

The first mention of Nietzsche links him with Ibsen. A girlviolinist, whose fiancé, a nobleman has insisted that she become a Catholic before their marriage, suggests to her betrothed that he read Ibsen and Nietzsche.[6] Here Nietzsche clearly stands for antichurch liberalism.

Nietzsche is twice referred to in the important converversation between Georg and Dr. Stauber in which they discuss plans for the delivery of Anna's child. The wise and kindly old physician reveals his familiarity with modern views but indicates to Georg that fatherhood has always involved an element of responsibility. Nietzsche and Ibsen are cited by Stauber as examples of the modern moralities he has in mind[7]. Interestingly enough, however, Stauber does not then condemn Nietzsche as one might expect under such conditions, but rather praises him as belonging to those geniuses who had the courage of their convictions. At the same time, Stauber regards him as historically conditioned and limited:

> Soll ich Ihnen was sagen, Herr Baron? Es gibt über
> haupt keine neuen Ideen. Neue Gedankenintensi-

100

täten – das ja. Aber meinen Sie im Ernst, dass
Nietzsche den Übermenschen, Ibsen, die Lebens-
lüge erfunden hat, und Anzengruber die Wahrheit,
dass die Eltern selber „danach sein sollen", die von
ihren Kindern Verehrung und Liebe wünschen?
Keine Spur. Alle ethischen Ideen sind immer dage-
wesen, und staunen würde man, wenn man wüsste,
was für Flachköpfe die sogenannten neuen, grossen
Wahrheiten gedacht, vielleicht sogar manchmal
ausgesprochen haben, lang vor den Genies, denen
wir diese Wahrheiten verdanken, oder vielmehr den
Mut, diese Wahrheiten für wahr zu halten.[8]

Stauber regards Nietzsche as a truth-seeking genius and the
superman ideal as an ethical truth. However, he is unwilling
to accept the extreme implications of any ethical system,
since he feels that the new ethical ideas are not really new,
have always been with us, and so do not alter the facts of life.
When Stauber heard Anna's tale, there came into his mind,
he said, the old-fashioned words roué, seduction, desertion;[9]
these, too, he implied, were truths that could not be ignored.

Perhaps to set off the older Stauber's common-sense ethic
of human kindness, young Bertold Stauber advocates with
Nietzschean extremism that pity be disregarded:

Das Mitleid – und was kann Liebe zu Leuten, die
man nicht persönlich kennt, am Ende anderes sein
– führt notwendig zu Sentimentalität, zu Schwäche.
Und gerade, wenn man ganzen Menschengruppen
helfen will, muss man gelegentlich hart sein können gegen den einzelnen, ja muss imstande sein ihn
zu opfern, wenn's das allgemeine Wohl verlangt.[10]

Where does Schnitzler stand? Obviously, with the sensible old
doctor and not with the embittered, resentful young Berthold
who, his father feels, has become fanatically obsessed with his

ideas: "du fängst an, dich in deine Ideen zu verbohren."[11] But, on the other hand, Schnitzler had, as we say, two souls in his breast, and it would appear that he was not unwilling to give the superman ideal serious consideration under certain conditions, namely as the ethic of the creative artist. The way in which Georg Wergenthin is portrayed is a case in point, but to present the idea most clearly, let us first discuss a serious play, one of Schnitzler's best, written the same year in which *Der Weg ins Freie* was begun, 1903. This play, *Der einsame Weg*, has among its characters an amoral artist, an aging Anatol, named Julian Fichtner who like Georg seduces a girl and then leaves her in the lurch to pursue his career. It is our feeling that in the way he has presented this character, Schnitzler shows cognizance and partial acceptance of the superman ethics.

Fichtner justifies his desertion on the grounds that marriage would have meant an end to his career, and he admits without remorse that he would have felt his flight justified even if Gabriele had commited suicide. Here the Nietzschean dogma of ethical egotism is presented in unmistakable terms.

To digress slightly for a moment, it is not at all unlikely that Schnitzler had Nietzsche in mind when he wrote the play, for it contains numerous other Nietzschean motifs. For example, Dr. Reumann voices a Nietzschean tenet when he articulates a basic theme in the drama, namely that a lie which fosters life is superior to a truth which is detrimental to life.[12] His disdain for "Betrogene und Betrüger" as merely the "maskierter Neid" of one who would have liked to lead an unconventional life, whether uttered with tongue-in-cheek or not, brings to mind Nietzsche's famed "ressentiment" of the weak.[13] Like Reumann, Professor Wegrat also yearns at times for a life of amoral self-assertion: "das Leben strömte mächtig hin; man musste nur etwas frecher sein und selbstbewusster sich hineinwerfen."[14]

Wegrat envies Fichtner and wishes that he could be like

him; yet at the same time he realizes that they are totally different individuals. Himself he classifies rather harshly but not inaccurately as a "Beamte," whereas he considers Fichtner to belong to those geniuses who live in a world of their own and are beyond discussion like the elements[15], an obvious rephrasing of the idea of the artistic superman beyond good and evil.

Not of least importance, the somber pessimism of the play is more profound than in any earlier Schnitzler drama and has the full heavy tone of Nietzschean nihilism.

However, whether *Der Weg ins Freie* was directly influenced by Nietzsche must, for the present at least, still remain conjecture. What is crystal clear is that Schnitzler in this drama was putting the Nietzschean ethic to the test. What does he conclude? That in some cases, perhaps, the ethic is justified.

Many critics feel that Schnitzler damned Fichtner and justify their argument by pointing out that his son renounced him for his unselfish foster-father. This latter fact is indeed true and Fichtner is condemned to an old-age of loneliness. But is not every other character in the play, including the well-meaning and slightly pedantic Wegrat, who is far less an artist than even Fichtner, including Gabriele, Johanna, von Sala, Dr. Reumann and Irene condemned to a like fate? Do they not all suffer the inevitable fate of loneliness? That is the tragic theme of the play. Loneliness is the inevitable destiny of all human beings.

If one looks closely, it is apparent that Schnitzler shows a large measure of affection and understanding for the amoral Fichtner. Von Sala, a Schnitzler spokesman, says with sincerity, if with a trace of his usual flippant irony, that he considers Fichtner one of his closest friends. Schnitzler presents Fichtner at all times as sincere and forthright, never as hypocritical. He is sincerely bereaved at the news of Gabriele's demise; he is truly fond of his son; he tells Felix the story of the desertion honestly and without false sentimentality, admitting that the days after he had left the unfortunate Gabriele were among the happiest and most successful in his life. Schnitzler leans over backward to justify Fichtner's conduct, by indicating that he had drifted into the affair almost without knowing that he had done so, had glided into a beautiful dream from which he had suddenly awakened into cold reality the night before the elopement. He had found himself faced with a great decision and had decided that to be untrue to himself would have caused greater unhappiness to all concerned than it would have if he had yielded to pity. Schnitzler's deep interest in Fichtner and the complexity of the character are evident in the fact that the dramatist insisted to Brahm that only a certain capable actor be allowed to play the role.[16]

To recapitulate: Schnitzler seems to have justified Fichtner's ruthless desertion in terms of his personality and goal. One may perhaps assert that Schnitzler did not affirm immoralism and restricted himself to the psychological portrayal of the artist-type. We would have no fault to find with this statement, as we do not mean that Schnitzler condoned Fichtner's conduct any more than Stauber was pleased by Georg's frivolity. But the dramatist seems to be saying that egotism is a characteristic of the artist, a necessary characteristic, and must be accepted as such.

Let us return now to Georg Wergenthin. He has no feelings of remorse when he leaves Anna for good. The closing lines of the novel read:

> In Georgs Seele war ein mildes Abschiednehmen
> von mancherlei Glück und Leid, die er in dem Tal,
> das er nun für lange verliess, gleichsam verhallen
> hörte; und zugleich ein Grüssen unbekannter Tage,
> die aus der Weite der Welt seiner Jugend entgegen-
> klangen.[17]

Was Georg at fault? His friend, the keen intellectual, Heinrich

Bermann, tells him that he was not. For another person his act might well have involved guilt, but for him who was "von Natur aus – verzeihen Sie – ziemlich leichtfertig und ein bisschen gewissenlos angelegt...war es gewiss nicht Schuld."[18]

Is there not a tacit condemnation in the failure of Fichtner and Wergenthin to become great artists? We believe not. Fichtner achieved more as an artist than the kindly Wegrat; Wergenthin is told by Bermann that whereas he is not destined to be a great creative artist, a composer, he has a real mission as a musical director in correctly reproducing great music for the people at large.[19]

In a sense, Wergenthin and Fichtner are less superman than half-heroes; yet they are both true artist-types whose character and way of life demand an egotistical pursuit of their own interest. They are doomed to pay the price with loneliness, but they are justified in remaining true to their own nature; this is what Schnitzler seems to be saying, and this is the extent to which we believe he accepted the Nietzschean code of ethics.

Only two further references to Nietzsche came to our attention: in *Der Puppenspieler* (1902) reference is made to the Nietzsche slogan, "Jenseits von Gut und Böse," and in *Das weite Land* (1910), the pianist, Korsakow, was described as being learned by noting his familiarity with the views of Kant, Schopenhauer, Nietzsche, and Proudhon. Here Nietzsche is treated as a philosopher rather than as a moralist, and it would be enlightening with more data at hand, to consider whether by 1910 his interest in Nietzsche had broadened to his philosophy, papticulary to the latter's views on the relativity of truth.

With our facts exhausted, it is time to draw final conclusions. It is evident that Schnitzler was familiar with Nietzsche's ethics and presumably had read at least *Also sprach Zarathustra*, Nietzsche's most popular work which was read by millions of Europeans at the beginning of the century, and which in its first half deals largely with the doctrine of the superman. It would appear that Schnitzler's concern with the *Herrenmoral* reached its peak around 1903, as at this time his writings reveal a new ethical revaluation of the amoral artist. Schnitzler seems to have decided that the *Herrenmoral* was the correct and proper expression of the artistic personality, perhaps even of his own personality, but he was not willing to accept the Nietzschean ethic as a universal guide for human conduct.

We do not believe, when all the facts about Schnitzler are known, that his relationship to Nietzsche the moralist will be materially different from that which we have shown; however, it is possible, even likely, that a linkage with Nietzsche's philosophy, particularly his theory of knowledge, may be established.

NOTES

[1] Arthur Schnitzler, *Gesammelte Werke, Die Theaterstücke* (Berlin, S. Fischer) vol. 4, 190-191.

[2] Kurt Bergel, *Georg Brandes und Arthur Schnitzler. Ein Briefwechsel*, University of California Publications in Modern Philology, vol. 46, 29-30.

[3] *Ibid.*

[4] Oskar Seidlin, *Der Briefwechsel Arthur Schnitzler-Otto Brahm* (Berlin, 1953). After making the comments in question, Schnitzler comes to speak about the progress he has made in his novel!

[5] *Der Weg ins Freie* is a *Schlüsselroman* and Georg was modelled by Schnitzler after a known prototype. The fact remains, however, that Georg also represents one facet of Schnitzler's outlook and personality.

[6] Arthur Schnitzler, *Der Weg Ins Freie* (Berlin, 1928), 143.

[7] *Ibid.*, 203.

[8] *Ibid.*, 203-204.

[9] *Ibid.*, 204.

[10] *Ibid.*, 387.

[11] *Ibid.*, 385.

[12] Cf. fn. 1, vol. 3, p. 29.

[13] *Ibid.*, 28.

[14] *Ibid.*, 69.

[15] *Ibid.*, 26.

[16] Cf. fn. 4.

[17] Cf. fn. 6, p 460. It should be noted that Heinrich Bermann in *Der Weg ins Freie*, writer, intellectual and Schnitzler spokesman, has a similar affair. The deserted girl commits suicide. Bermann is distraught, yet he says he does not feel guilty and would in a similar situation act in the same fashion. "Es durfte nicht sein. Ein Verbrechen wär es gewesen, dieses todkranke Verhältnis weiterzufristen..." (p. 439). Anna considers Bermann "ein schauerlicher Egoist." (p. 248).

[18] *Ibid.*, 458. From the whole opera concerning Ägidius, the author reveals that Georg is the fortunate and yet tragically doomed hero. "Ein Todgeweihter." (p. 311).

[19] *Ibid.*, 408.

OBSERVATIONS ON SCHNITZLER'S NARRATIVE TECHNIQUES IN THE SHORT NOVEL

by Robert Donald Spector

While even the best literary critics have been unable to define adequately the *short story, novella*, and *novel*, they generally agree about placing individual works within a genre and acknowledge a common ground for certain characteristics. No one was seriously misled when Hemingway's *Old Man and the Sea* was transplanted from its rather cramped space in *Life* magazine to the fulness of a Scribners' edition which had the most generous margins in recent book publishing. Moreover, an examination of the effect of Hemingway's work clearly reveals that, for all its prolixity, it is no more than a short story. In the same way, Mann's *Death in Venice*, Flaubert's *A Simple Heart*, and Tolstoy's *The Death of Iván Ilých* are easily recognizable as *novellas*. Despite their unity, these works have thematic development, character analyses, and varied detail that take them beyond the limits of the short story, and yet their unity is of a kind far too specific for the novel.

The question of genre, however insoluble, is worthy of consideration, for it frequently leads to an understanding of the reasons for success or failure in a particular work. There are things that a short story should not attempt to do. When it seeks, for example, to go outside the limits of its primary incidents, it becomes flaccid and dissipates its necessary impact. By the same token, the *novella* that emphasizes its plot and so tries to gain its effect through these surface narrative devices concludes in superficiality.

Perhaps nowhere are the distinctions between the short story and *novella* to be better drawn than in the work of Schnitzler which appeared in an American translation called *Viennese Novelettes.** Through the successes and failures of five stories – *Daybreak* (*Spiel im Morgengrauen*), *Fräulein Else*, *Rhapsody* (*Traumnovelle*), *Beatrice* (*Frau Beate*), and *"None but the Brave"* (*Leutnant Gustl*) – the effects of appropriate genres may be traced. Where Schnitzler stays within the framework of a genre, the result is rewarding; where he strays – generally for the sake of fashionable appeal – he loses the effectiveness of his art. Yet there is as much to be learned from the one as from the other.

Indeed, what the opening story teaches comes through its ultimate failure. Because Schnitzler is undecided about its genre, *Daybreak* combines two narrative techniques and fails to satisfy with either. The pace is leisurely, too leisurely for the short story form although appropriate enough for the *novella*. But by plunging into his action, Schnitzler, at first, gives the impression that he is writing a short story. This illusion is maintained in Lieutenant Kasda's initial comments on the absurdity of the erstwhile Lieutenant Bogner's conduct in permitting himself to be destroyed by his gambling impulse. Kasda's statement and its tone are a clear foreshadowing of his own experience, and were the narritave to end with Kasda's defeat at the card table, it would generally meet that requirement of the short form which calls for one major change of circumstance.

Yet everything else in Schnitzler's method along the way indicates that he is attempting something beyond the perfunctory well-made narrative. In his treatment of the gam-

* Arthur Schnitzler, *Viennese Novelettes* (New York, 1931).

110

bling episode, Schnitzler uses details and devices that go to extremes too bulky for the short story. The gradual development of Kasda's circumstances, the interplay of fate and character that leads him to his debacle, and the long sideglances at the affairs of others belong to the technique of the *novella*. Even after the gambling loss, Schnitzler covers territory that lies outside the realm of the short story. Indeed, were he determined to stay within those bounds, the later material (such as Kasda's affair with his uncle's wife, the recollection of their earlier liaison, and the uncle's decline in fortune) would be anticlimactic. Moreover, it is apparent from Schnitzler's interest in characterization – best expressed in the insights into Kasda's thoughts during the card game – that the author is essaying more than can properly be accomplished in the short story.

However, Schnitzler, who is at his best when he depreciates external action, here depends too much on the devices of plot to be successful in the longer form. The tricks of fate, particularly at the conclusion when Kasda's uncle arrives too late to save him from suicide and momentarily has his suspicions aroused about his nephew's last night with his wife, belong to the tradition of the De Maupassant tale with its ironic if somewhat unbelievable twist. The fact, too, that Kasda succeeds in his initial purpose to save Bogner from prosecution for fraud and yet is destroyed himself in the effort has the grim humor of an O. Henry story. Were any of these the termination of a shorter narrative, it would no doubt be effective, but the necessary vigor is lost as Schnitzler covers a larger compass of ground. To be sure, there is much that is admirable in *Daybreak*, especially the realism of Kasda's desperation at the card table, but narrative technique that is inappropriate to content minimizes the effectiveness of any work of art.

The art comes close to its utmost satisfaction, however, in Schnitzler's second story in the collection. Like Lieutenant Kasda, the heroine of *Fräulein Else* is destroyed in saving someone else – in this instance, her father – from the consequences of improvident gambling. She must approach the lecherous old man Dorsday to attempt a loan that will keep her parent from prison and her family from disgrace. Throughout the story, Schnitzler is concerned, as he was in *Daybreak*, with the social hypocrisies, the false codes of honor, and the dualities of character. Yet *Fräulein Else* is a triumph of art because it adapts form to content as *Daybreak* did not.

External action in itself is truly of little consequence to Schnitzler here. Its function is to provide the surface tensions against which the normal and confused sexuality of young Else's development is distorted and perverted into the neurotic hysterical behavior that terminates in her suicide. Given the restrictions of the short story form, the necessary repetition of detail and the subtleties of distinction at various stages would clutter the narrative. In the larger area of the *novella*, they perform a rhythmical function that provides depth and unity to the work. It is a poetic device applied naturally enough to a prose work that bears a close resemblance to the dramatic monologue. As details are repeated, they recall their former use, and yet their slight alterations suggest a progression in the character's point of view. Upon Else's first meeting with Dorsday before her own fate is linked to him, she speaks objectively of his calves' eyes, but when she seeks him out for help, it becomes, "What calves' eyes he is making at me!" What has happened between the two occasions – Dorsday's being proposed as the man who can save her father – has turned the quite innocent comment into a personal appraisal. In the same way, Else's observations of Paul, Cissy, her aunt, father, mother, and brother undergo a subtle transition as her circumstances change. For Schnitzler in *Fräulein Else* that fact rather than the plot development is important.

Gone is the trick ending, which, if Schnitzler had been writing the well-made short story, would have offered Else's view of those around her as being ironically inaccurate. Instead, the affair that she has suspected between her cousin Paul and Cissy is verified before her apparently senseless form, and the callousness that she has instinctively felt in others is demonstrated at her very deathbed.

While the bizarre events in the surface narrative of *Rhapsody* are intriguing and carry their own suspense, Schnitzler in this third story is employing them as a device for examining the depths of his characters. To be sure, there is more of the quality of the facile short story in *Raphsody* than in *Fräulein Else*, and its conclusion – the moment of revelation in the morgue – provides an epiphany that is characteristic of that genre. Nevertheless, the exploration of the boundaries between reality and illusion is less concerned with the plot resolution, typical of the short story, than it is with the functioning of a particular mind, natural material for a *novella*. If in *Fräulein Else* Schnitzler happily applied the techniques of stream-of-consciousness to his psychological case study, in *Rhapsody* he demonstrates that fantasy can be used for the same purpose.

Perhaps it will help to distinguish between the *novella* that Schnitzler has written and the material as it would have appeared in the short story. Had *Rhapsody* been a short story, it might have opened with the same situation that Schnitzler has used: a husband and wife reactivated in their marriage through separate flirtations at a masquerade ball. From that point on, however, the selectivity imposed on a short story writer would have limited the areas of development open to Schnitzler. The theme of jealousy, the subtle description of a double standard, the character distinctions between the married couple, all would have been jettisoned in the need to carry the single effect that is expected from the short story. Schnitzler would have been required to discard the experiences with the costumer's daughter, the frustrations with both Marianne and the prostitute, in order to concentrate on the incredible episode of the naked ladies at the mystery ball. As a matter of fact, even the irresolution of Schnitzler's conclusion would require alternation as the finish to a short story since the change that is effected is no change at all but rather the acceptance of the variety of experiences through which the character has passed. For the *novella*, where impact and suspense are adjuncts and not requisites, such a conclusion is appropriate; for the short story, seeking primarily an emotional response, it is not.

It is a *novella* that Schnitzler has written. Its burden is again a play between the surface tensions and the emotional disturbances of the hero. Schnitzler, familiar with Freud, makes use of Freudian dream techniques and symbolic devices to delineate character, to support motivation, and to explain conduct. Within the narrow confines of a short story, much of this detail would appear superfluous; in a *novella* it becomes as much an end in itself as a method of narration.

In order to transmute his Freudian material to art in *Beatrice*, the next story, Schnitzler is again compelled to make use of the *novella*. The narrative is composed of several stages in the development of the heroine: from the chaste widow, living in dedication to a false ideal, to a passionate fool, deceiving herself about her real desires, to a tragic figure, yielding to her incestuous drives and to death. Each step requires background, motivation, and detail. Each change supplies its own climax. While the particular kind of character unity rules out the possibility of a novel, it is too varied to be satisfied by the form of a short story, and only the middle ground of the *novella* will do.

Action is again less a matter of narrative than of mind, and Schnitzler displays an unusual talent for capturing the sensitivity of a feminine point of view. Whereas in *Fräulein Else* he presented the workings of a young girl's thought process, difficult enough in itself, here he takes on the burden of the sophistications that embroider the thinking of a mature

114

woman. In *Fraulein Else* he was able to use the stream-of-consciousness technique, far more adaptable to an exposition of the mind than ordinary narrative and dramatic devices are. The problems in *Beatrice*, however, do not allow for the same narrative method. He cannot have Beatrice conscious of her incestuous impulses without giving the game away, but instead he must use a limited omniscience which makes clear her point of view and yet suggests to the reader what is shaping her actions, what accounts for her conduct, and what devices help her to hide the truth from herself.

Once more the leisurely pace of the *novella* permits him the opportunity to deal with observations that are less essential to the narrative than they are congenial to his comments on society and types of individuals. It affords him the chance to paint portraits of the wanton woman, living through her deceptions, youth in the boastfulness of its conquests, and middle age envying the opportunities of the young. To be sure, these play a role in Schnitzler's action, but they would be a handicap in the limited form of the short story, while they enhance the credibility and lend fulness to the *novella*.

Schnitzler's final story in the collection – *"None but the Brave"* – has been regarded as one of his early masterpieces, and despite the weakness of a *deus ex machina* conclusion, it is truly a remarkable achievement in the early development of a stream-of-consciousness technique. Yet it is important to recognize that the work is a short story rather than a novella. Not only is its length considerably less than what one expects in the latter genre, but the very psychology that molds its form provides a unity consistent with the short story rather than the *novella*. To be sure, there is implied comment on the military code and values – an implication strong enough to have cost Schnitzler his commission in the medical reserves – and there are suggestions of Lieutenant Gustl's emotional involvements outside the particular episode. Nevertheless, these are not developed with the kind of adequacy that would be

115

necessary in the longer form; they are not, for example, given the same stress that they received in *Fräulein Else*, although the techniques of the two stories otherwise invite comparison.

What Schnitzler is attempting to show in *"None but the Brave"* is a particular *state* of mind. Were it not so, the story would be a failure. As it is, the trick ending, while common enough in the genre, is trying and is acceptable only because it is inconsequential to Schnitzler's purpose in the narrative. The entire affair of the insult from the baker is, in fact, a kind of subterfuge that the lieutenant has created to divert his mind from his impending duel with the doctor. The contemplated suicide is a mental ruse to permit an individual confronted with the uncertainties of one adventure to seek another in which he may captain his own fate by marshalling his own circumstances. The sudden death of the baker would prove ruinous to a short story were it to be the main object of the narrative; to a *novella* it would be altogether inappropriate because of the kind of climax it produces.

The suggestion that Schnitzler presents the lieutenant's "most intimate thoughts with all the relevant and irrelevant associations of ideas" is positively misleading. It is an attempt to describe the work as a *novella*, rich with the sort of detail that lends breadth to a vision of life that can be properly explored in the genre. Yet any careful reading of Schnitzler's story indicates that the details are never irrelevant. The fastening on to things that are sensuous, the attachment to earlier experiences provide a counterpoint to the present fears. Like the Blakean romantic who seizes a tree to assure himself of reality, Lieutenant Gustl conjures up those images that seem assurances against death. Whatever the seemingly rambling quality of his thoughts, they bear with a determined unity upon his particular circumstance. As such, they lend to the appropriateness of the genre that Schnitzler has chosen, and *"None but the Brave"* is evidence that he could master the short story, just as *Beatrice* attests to his skill in the *novella*.